To Debbie —

Mystery book always
take you where you
want to go !

10/29/22

Reflections on *Daingerfield Island* by John Adam Wasowicz

I wandered into Antidote Books in Putney, Vermont, not long ago in search of a useful diversion for the Christmas holiday and there upon the new arrivals table was "Daingerfield Island" by John Wasowicz.

I'll admit it, I was initially drawn to the book by its cover, a snap judgment, if you will. Equally intriguing, I knew Mr. Wasowicz long ago when we were both burning thru our parents' savings as college students. I knew that John had abandoned New England many years previously for Washington, D.C., which is where the trail ran cold. Although I've never dwelled on it, never would it have occurred to me that he'd take pen in hand, so to speak, and actually turn life into art.

I dabble occasionally in literature, and appropriately perhaps, I regard Raymond Chandler as among the greatest of American authors. No one ever set a scene better; think of Philip Marlowe entering General Sternwood's sweltering orchid room. The humidity and cloying scent of the orchids overwhelming Marlowe even before he first glimpses the elderly and infirm Sternwood wrapped in blankets and propped up in a wheelchair. It's literature, not just escapist fiction. Chandler is the bar by which I judge American writing.

Now where does that leave the novice writer in a modern world in which content seems to completely outrun the opportunity to absorb it? It's a high bar, and in "Daingerfield Island" Mr. Wasowicz has surmounted it first time out of the gate. Elmo Katz, the defense lawyer who has to take divorce work to survive, something the principled Philip Marlowe won't do, accepts the defense of a murder suspect with ties to the CIA who might in turn be involved in a much larger national security scenario, all of which turns on a random piece of evidence recovered by a random passerby at an apparent murder scene.

It's a masterfully plotted page-turner in the grand manner of detective fiction, so well done in fact, that what seems obvious really isn't, even when you've correctly identified the clues, and that is no small accomplishment. I read the book cover to cover between breakfast and very late Christmas dinner, putting the book down only when it was absolutely necessary.

David Clark, Westminster, VT, December 2018

Praise for *Jones Point* by John Adam Wasowicz

"A FOLLOW-UP TO *DAINGERFIELD ISLAND*, *Jones Point* is masterfully crafted, keeping even the protagonists guessing. I couldn't put it down."
–Thomas Lyons, owner and operator of The New England Mobile Book Fair, Newton, MA

"*JONES POINT* IS A WINNER, a thriller of our times that grows out of the real Washington, DC, where decent people do the best they can to keep the rest of us safe. Highly recommended."
–Jake Needham, author of the Barry Award nominated *Samuel Tay* series.

"MO KATZ AND CREW take on assorted miscreants in this kinetic thriller. A real page-turner!"
–Dayna Wilkinson, DC Chapter Head, Harvardwood

"A FAST-PACED, COMPELLING MURDER MYSTERY that races to an action-packed climax. Clever plotting keeps the reader guessing. Suspenseful to the end."
–Nancy A. Olson, poet and freelance writer, Putney, VT

"ABSOLUTELY SATISFYING! It was fantastic to slip back into Mo Katz's world with his cast of supporting characters. Wasowicz has delivered another suspenseful whodunit, weaving politics, conspiracy, and murder together for a can't-put-it-down tale."
–Angela S. Shores, PhD, owner and operator of Adventure Bound Books, Morganton, NC

"BUMPS UP AGAINST RAYMOND CHANDLER, but without so many of Marlowe's zingers."
–Brooke C. Stoddard, author of *Steel: From Mine to Mill, the Metal that Made America*

"WASOWICZ WILL HOOK YOU FROM THE VERY BEGINNING! I was thoroughly entertained."
–PeggySue Jenkins, Store Manager, Book Warehouse, Gettysburg, PA

Also by John Adam Wasowicz

Daingerfield Island

JONES POINT

by

John Adam Wasowicz

JONES POINT

Publisher: Clarinda Harriss
Editor: Charles Rammelkamp
Graphic Design: Ace Kieffer
Author Photo: Aron J. Wasowicz
Cover Art and Map: Alex Herron Wasowicz

BrickHouse Books, Inc. 2019
306 Suffolk Road
Baltimore, MD 21218

Distributor: Itasca Books, Inc.

ISBN: 978-1-938144-63-9

Printed in the United States of America

To RT

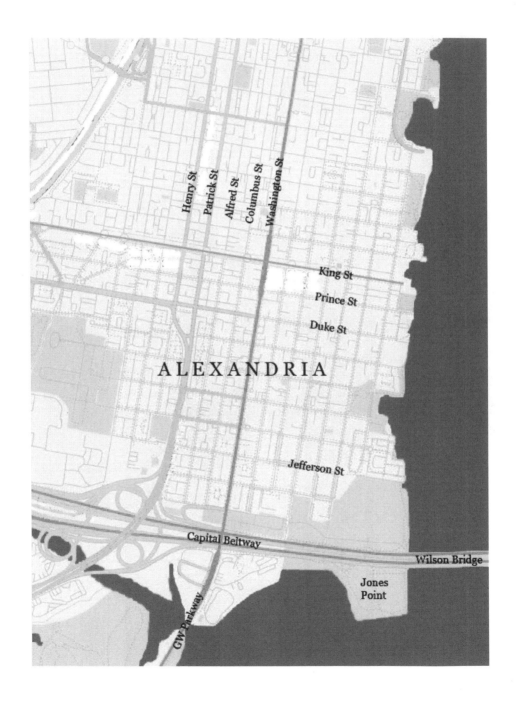

"The year is full of warnings of its shortness, as is life."

– Henry David Thoreau

TABLE OF CONTENTS

PROLOGUE 15

CHAPTER 1 17

CHAPTER 2 20

CHAPTER 3 25

CHAPTER 4 29

CHAPTER 5 30

CHAPTER 6 35

CHAPTER 7 38

CHAPTER 8 42

CHAPTER 9 44

CHAPTER 10 49

CHAPTER 11 53

CHAPTER 12 56

CHAPTER 13 60

CHAPTER 14 63

CHAPTER 15 65

CHAPTER 16 67

CHAPTER 17 71

CHAPTER 18 74

CHAPTER 19 76

CHAPTER 20 79

CHAPTER 21 84

CHAPTER 22 88

CHAPTER 23 91

CHAPTER 24 94

CHAPTER 25 99

CHAPTER 26 104

CHAPTER 27 107

CHAPTER 28 109

CHAPTER 29 111

CHAPTER 30 115

CHAPTER 31 117

CHAPTER 32 120

CHAPTER 33 122

CHAPTER 34 126

CHAPTER 35 130

CHAPTER 36 134

CHAPTER 37 137

CHAPTER 38 139

CHAPTER 39 143

CHAPTER 40 147

CHAPTER 41 150

CHAPTER 42 154

CHAPTER 43 158

CHAPTER 44 161

CHAPTER 45 164

CHAPTER 46 169

CHAPTER 47 174

CHAPTER 48 177

CHAPTER 49 179

CHAPTER 50 183

CHAPTER 51 186

CHAPTER 52 191

CHAPTER 53 194

CHAPTER 54 200

CHAPTER 55 203

CHAPTER 56 206

CHAPTER 57 210

CHAPTER 58 213

CHAPTER 59 216

CHAPTER 60 221

CHAPTER 61 223

CHAPTER 62 227

CHAPTER 63 231

EPILOGUE 232

AUTHOR'S NOTE 234

ACKNOWLEDGEMENT 235

PROLOGUE

A full moon illuminated a milky sky. Ten miles south of the nation's capital, cars and trucks glided across the Wilson Bridge, their headlights shining like diamonds. A dirty gray Dodge Magnum swung around a corner in Old Town Alexandria and stopped beneath the bridge at the end of a long, wide parking lot at the tip of Jones Point. Overhead, the illuminated massive white arches of the bridge rose like the hands of a god cradling ribbons of asphalt across the Potomac River between Virginia and Maryland.

The car's driver doused the lights and popped the hatch. Then he and another man exited the vehicle and walked around to the back. The two men, both burly and with close-cropped black hair, yanked a body from the cargo area and tossed it carelessly on the blacktop. The body, caked in dry blood, landed against a bollard planted at the far perimeter of the parking area.

The driver paused for a moment to finish the cigarette dangling from the corner of his mouth, then tossed the butt to the pavement.

In silence, the two men grabbed the body, one taking the hands and the other the legs, and carried it twenty yards across dead grass to the pier that jutted out into the water. They walked a few more yards onto the pier and then heaved the limp form into the river. As the body hit the water, waves slapped against the pilings.

The gears of an eighteen-wheeler groaned overhead. The men looked up at the bridge. Lights at the base of its V-shaped supports transformed the bridge into a monument as distinctive as the Lincoln Memorial or the Washington Monument.

"We go, Alec," the driver growled.

The men ambled to the car. The driver's and passenger's doors opened simultaneously and slammed in unison with the grace of a choreographed scene. The car's lights turned on, its beams stabbing the night. The vehicle retreated from Jones Point, turned right onto a quiet residential street and disappeared, leaving behind only a strong odor of gasoline.

CHAPTER 1

Two weeks earlier.

A slight drizzle fell as U.S. Attorney Elmo Katz slipped into the Lyceum. He grabbed an hors d'oeuvre from a silver tray and washed it down with a six-ounce bottle of sparkling water. Then he worked his way through the crowd until he found a lithe blonde standing by herself and observing the festivities.

"Where did you come from?" Abby Snowe asked without turning toward him as he slid beside her like a warm breeze. She tilted her head in his direction. They exchanged a soft kiss.

"Just got here," he whispered.

Without asking, she knew another unscheduled meeting on the Bank of Magellan case had scuttled his plans for an early exit from the office, even on the Friday before the Labor Day weekend.

Snowe and Katz stood quietly inside a white, columned, classical structure a block from the main intersection of King and Washington Streets in Old Town Alexandria that served as a cultural center for musical and artistic performances. Though he'd driven by it hundreds of times, Katz had never stepped inside the building until tonight.

"Who would have thought Mo Katz would be so engrossed in a civil case," Snowe smiled knowingly.

"It's the bomb," he replied, playing off the acronym – BOM – the prosecutor's office team used to describe the Bank of Magellan case.

He grabbed another appetizer from a tray balanced in a waiter's hand.

"People missed you at the courthouse," Snowe said, referring to the award ceremony recognizing Alexandria Police Detective Sherry Stone for valor. Snowe spoke in a chastising tone that suggested Katz had a responsibility to be punctual.

Katz shrugged and adjusted his striped blue tie. Dressed in a blue seersucker suit and pink shirt, he looked cool, despite the steamy weather outside. His prematurely grizzled hair, with a texture like steel wool, was cut short and glistened under the artificial lights. His white teeth sparkled as he smiled at Snowe.

His first name – Elmo – was a composite of data points in the lives of his parents, Myron Katz, a Jew born in Brooklyn, and Denise Wells, an African American from the Motor City. They met as students at the University of Chicago in the late '70s. "El" stood for the Chicago Transit Authority's train system, the "L," their preferred – their only – form of transportation in those days. "Mo" was for Motown Records, whose R&B tunes by Smokey Robinson and the Miracles and Diana Ross and the Supremes provided the musical backdrop of their romance.

After earning a law degree at Georgetown, Katz settled in Virginia, taking a job as a city assistant commonwealth attorney. Three years of handling prosecutions ranging from minor traffic offenses to capital murder gave way to the so-called dark side, a criminal defense practice. Then, two years ago, he was selected U.S. Attorney for the Eastern District of Virginia after untangling a complex terrorist-related case that began with a murder off Daingerfield Island, south of Reagan National Airport.

To Katz, the office was not a stepping-stone to higher office but rather an opportunity to do some good. But that wasn't something he shared with others for fear he would sound too altruistic, too off-message for a former maverick defense attorney. After all, he had a reputation to maintain.

"You should work the room," Snowe instructed. "Come on." Slim and champagne pale, and dressed in ballet flats and a flowing teal dress, she moved like a rani leading her entourage, preceding Katz to where Stone greeted well-wishers. Sometimes Katz wondered whether Snowe, a veteran in the city's probation office, possessed political ambitions for both of them.

Katz and Stone embraced warmly, touching cheeks. "Right on time," she cooed. Stone's warm brown face was accentuated by her eyes, inscrutable and unforgiving. Her facial structure was on the masculine side: hard square chin, firm cheekbones, and aquiline nose. She wore her hair natural and cut short, shaved at the sides and thicker on top. While she usually wore conservative gold studs, tonight she was wearing gold hoop earrings that nearly reached her shoulders.

"I wouldn't have missed it for the world," Katz replied. "After all, you're a hero. A slightly different set of circumstances and children could have died."

He referred to Stone's unscheduled visit to pick up her niece at a daycare center, a twist of fate that put her face-to-face with an angry father in the throes of a heated custody dispute. When he unexpectedly pulled out a handgun in a room filled with crayons, coloring books, and tiny plastic chairs, she calmly told him to drop it. When he refused, and as stunned parents and preschoolers watched, she employed her black belt skills to kick the weapon out of his hand and take him to the floor.

"They mint badges for people like you," Katz said. "Great turnout," he added, looking around.

The room overflowed with many people who had planned to be outside the Beltway for a last reprieve before autumn's arrival. Schedules had been scratched or reshuffled by the region's high-powered elites, including judges, members of the Virginia General Assembly, the mayor, the city council and the Northern Virginia congressional delegation, the chief of police, and a contingent of law enforcement officers from Alexandria and neighboring jurisdictions.

"They're here out of obligation," Stone replied modestly. "It's all about making an appearance, seeing and being seen."

Katz nodded, though he knew that was not the case in this instance. Stone had forged a path uniquely her own. In the process, she had gained a following of loyal fans and admirers.

They separated, and Katz and Snowe mingled with the crowd. He exchanged pleasantries with everyone in the room, but his mind was already elsewhere, thinking how to combine a criminal conviction with a civil remedy in the BOM case. The idea of settling a money-laundering case involving armaments that killed American soldiers for only civil damages was anathema to him.

After thirty minutes, Snowe and Katz bade farewell and withdrew hand-in-hand from the celebration, which showed no signs of winding down.

CHAPTER 2

"That wasn't so bad, was it?" Snowe asked as they stepped onto Washington Street. The drizzle had stopped. A thin sheen covered the sidewalk; the street appeared glazed in the streetlight. Overhead, clouds separated as sparkling stars appeared in a moonless sky.

Before Katz could answer, a man bumped his shoulder. Katz turned, annoyed. Then his face broke into a smile. He grabbed the man's suit sleeve. "Hey," he said, "Sean. Sean Matthews. How are you?"

The man's anxious expression relaxed slightly. "Mo, how the hell are you? I'm heading to Stoner's gig. I must really be late if you're already leaving."

Katz grinned. "It's just getting started," he said, then quickly did introductions.

"We've met," Snowe said coldly, wrapping her fingers around Katz's arm instead of shaking hands with Matthews.

"You're looking good," Katz said to Matthews, pivoting from the awkwardness of Snowe's rebuff. Hunched and disheveled in a rumpled suit, with a bushel of wheat-colored unkempt hair stacked atop his head, Matthews hardly appeared a figure worthy of compliment.

"I'm struggling," Matthews said bluntly, brushing off the insincere comment. "You remember what that was like, don't you?"

"I sure do," Katz laughed, recalling the vagaries of private practice.

Six years ago, Katz had briefly joined forces with Matthews after departing the Commonwealth Attorney's office. For a brief moment, the shingle outside Matthews' ramshackle law office building read "Matthews & Katz." In less than two months, however, Katz struck out on his own, dissatisfied with Matthews' lowbrow clientele. He launched a highly successful solo practice, culminating in his adroit handling of the Daingerfield Island case.

Matthews forced a smile as the same thoughts flickered through both their minds. *One career accelerated while the other stalled.*

"Pretty soon you'll be competing for your girlfriend's client base," Katz said.

"I'll never run a silk-stocking boutique, if that's what you mean," replied Matthews.

"She's giving us fits in the Magellan case, making us jump through all sorts of hoops."

Matthews stiffened. "I wouldn't know. Jane and I don't discuss work. That's not what our relationship is about." Then he added, "Fortunately, you're going to get a bit of a reprieve. We're headed to Columbia Bay now that the crowds are gone."

"When do you leave?" Katz asked casually.

"Sunday. I'm flying down to meet her. We'll spend a little over a week down south and come back on the ninth. She's got an engagement in your office on Thursday, the twelfth."

Katz knew all about it. "Give me a call when you get back." He affectionately patted Matthews' arm. "We've got a lot of catching up to do."

"Will do," Matthews said with a faint smile.

"Goodnight, my friend," Katz said as the rumpled figure turned away.

Katz and Snowe exchanged a glance as they strolled up King Street, the city's main thoroughfare, toward the Hard Times Café.

"That was awkward," Snowe said, chuckling.

"What can I say? Our lives took different trajectories."

"I wouldn't put it that way. Trajectory suggests flight." Snowe made an arc with her hand. "I don't think his career ever lifted off the launching pad."

"Whatever," Katz said glibly. "Sean's not a bad guy." He felt her stare. "So, what, did you have a bad Sean Matthews experience or something?"

"Yeah," she said. "As a matter of fact I did, a really bad one."

They arrived at the restaurant and ordered Texas chili and cornbread. As they ate, Snowe told her story. "I was the probation officer on a couple of his cases," she said. "He forged my name on some praecipes for favorable dispositions in criminal cases, including a couple of suspended imposition of sentence in cases where such an outcome is verboten."

It was common practice for prosecutors and defense attorneys to reach agreements in misdemeanor cases memorialized on a standard form called a praecipe. The forms were routinely used for first-time offenders for marijuana and minor offenses that allowed cases to be dismissed after one year if the defendant remained out of trouble and completed a drug rehabilitation program or other class ordered by a probation officer.

"You're kidding." Katz chuckled, though he actually felt what Matthews did was abhorrent. Forging a praecipe effectively destroyed the trust between prosecutor and defense attorney and technically constituted a crime. "What did you do?"

"I didn't report him, if that's what you're asking," she said. "But I never forgot it. Sean Matthews is a scumbag, and scumbags are the only people who seek him out for representation. They gravitate to him like fleas to a dog. I think they sense a kinship."

She dipped the cornbread into her bowl of chili. "You know it's true," she said. "It's why you broke your partnership with him. You never told me that, but I know it's why you did it."

Katz ate and said nothing.

Their conversation moved to personalities at the courthouse. Some judges were retiring while others were advancing from District to Circuit Court; the Circuit Court clerk was facing stiff opposition in the next election, as was the sheriff; and Stone's continued stellar performance on the force was positioning her as the city's next deputy chief of police.

"She's come a long way since back in the day," said Snowe.

"Stoner," Katz smiled.

Katz represented Stone on a cocaine charge when she was a rookie cop called Stevie. She would have crashed and burned but for Katz's courtroom machinations to nullify an otherwise valid criminal charge. She was an outcast on the force at the time, but Katz always liked and respected her. Katz got the case dismissed and she kept her job after a 30-day suspension, with pay. Out of gratitude, she referred to him tons of fellow officers needing legal representation in divorce cases and juvenile court cases involving their troubled kids.

As he finished eating, Katz asked, "Did you notice Matthews' expression when I mentioned the Magellan case?"

"It was so obvious," she said. "Like you had struck a nerve of some sort."

"I wasn't prying him for information, just paying Jane Hutton a compliment, you know."

A phone rang. An anxious expression crossed Snowe's face as she plucked the phone from her handbag and looked at the number. She rose awkwardly from the table and went outside.

"Is your mom okay?" he asked when she returned. Her face had lost color.

"She's dying," she replied matter-of-factly, sitting down. "What else am I supposed to say?"

They fell silent.

"We're all dying," he said.

Maybe time was running out, but Katz didn't want to talk about the things that were really in the back of their minds, like getting married and starting a family.

Eventually, Snowe picked up the thread of their conversation. "I don't think Matthews' behavior has anything to do with Hutton. Sure, he's jealous that she's such a successful lawyer while he's, well, perpetually stuck in a rut. But that's not it."

Their waitress arrived and dropped the check on the table.

"I think it's something else," Snowe continued. "Something sinister, in fact."

She did not elucidate. He did not pursue the comment. He felt the same way.

Eventually they wandered up King Street toward the Masonic Temple. Katz fell a few steps behind Snowe, glancing in store windows. She stopped, waiting for him. When he rejoined her, she asked, "Is everything alright?"

"Yeah," he said, although he could not help thinking that a slight twist of fate could have left him in the same stagnant pool of criminal defense work as Matthews for the rest of his professional life.

Their walk ended on the porch of his townhome on Harvard Street. A ceiling fan spun lazily overhead. Snowe sat in one of two white wicker chairs. He went inside and returned with two cold bottles of Port City lager. They sat drinking beer and watching an occasional car drive down the street.

It was after midnight when they went back inside. The evening air had turned cool. Autumn was fast approaching.

Katz stopped in the kitchen to clean the dishes left in the sink from last night's dinner. He also put away the spices Snowe had used to prepare the meal. "Are we out of thyme?" he asked, glancing at an empty container.

"I'm sorry," she said, stepping out of the small bathroom on the main level of the townhouse. "Are we out of what?" Then she spied the container in his hand.

He was reading the label on the bottle. "…distinctive flavor of its own…more complex when blended…"

She read the label over his shoulder. "Let's go upstairs and blend a few spices of our own," she said.

CHAPTER 3

Sean Matthews did not stay long at the Lyceum. He mingled with others, or tried to, but there was no place for him, no space between the lines for him to interject a witticism or make a joke. In truth, the well-heeled patrons at the awards ceremony had no use for him, a fly-by-the-seat-of-your-pants criminal defense attorney who took any case that walked in the door and probably had not studied the Virginia Code in 20 years.

He had no reason to go home. After all, Hutton had already departed for Columbia Bay. So he walked the few blocks to his office, a small wood-framed building at the end of an alley along Alfred Street.

Light shone from inside. Matthews thought that odd; he distinctly remembered buttoning up the office since he had planned to be away. He stood motionless for a moment beside a large dumpster at the edge of the building before proceeding cautiously up the rickety wooden steps to a rotting deck that led to the rear entrance. He unlocked the door and went inside.

A single lamp burned in the reception room. Matthews looked around suspiciously before retiring to his small office in the adjacent room, where he turned on the overhead lights. He immediately went to the desk drawer where he had stashed cash received from a client earlier in the week. The wad of bills was untouched. He retrieved the money and stuffed it inside his coat pocket.

He surveyed the office. Nothing appeared to have been disturbed. Convinced everything was in order, he turned off the lights, locked the door, went to his car, and drove to his apartment along the H Street corridor in D.C. Once there, he showered, drank some bourbon, and retired for the night. Before he fell asleep, however, his mind replayed a strange meeting with a new client earlier in the day.

**

The man was seated on the sofa in the otherwise unoccupied reception room. His hair was cut close. His expression was blank and his stare hollow. He was dressed in black: T-shirt, jacket, pants, socks, belt, and shoes.

As Matthews entered, the man stood, his spine stiff as a steel beam. "I am Boris Prolokov," he said with a slight foreign accent. "I would like to retain your services." Matthews noticed a bundle of files stacked on the sofa. Prolokov, following Matthews' eyes, added, "I have brought work with me."

Matthews invited Prolokov into his small, musty office. Prolokov retrieved the files and followed the attorney to the adjacent room. The desk was bare, with the exception of a few copies of court summons for criminal misdemeanors. Matthews rarely put his clients' papers in file folders, usually stuffing them in his pockets as he ran off to court. Once in court, he took whatever prosecutors offered to dispose of the cases, never bothering to go to trial. He wasn't there to challenge anybody; just make a fast buck and get out.

"Take a seat," said Matthews, pointing to two dilapidated chairs facing his desk. Prolokov frowned and selected the wooden swivel chair behind the desk. Matthews said nothing, taking one of the chairs facing the desk.

Prolokov dumped his files on the desk. "I own a business," he said. "A construction company. Pasha. You have heard of it?"

Matthews shook his head. "I can't say I have."

Prolokov opened one of the files and pulled out some brochures with PASHA in large letters on the covers. He slid them toward Matthews.

"It is a small operation." Prolokov raised his hand and opened a small space between his thumb and index finger. "A crumb compared to most construction firms."

Matthews nodded. After all, he reasoned, if Pasha was a reputable company, its CEO would not be visiting the Law Office of Sean Matthews, Esq., regardless of whether he sat in the chair behind the desk or not. There was no corporate counsel here. The corporate types were downtown along the K Street corridor, or in Bethesda or Tysons, the neighborhoods where Jane Hutton worked, and not down an alley in a hole-in-the-wall office.

"What can I do to help?"

"I need a registered agent in Virginia," Prolokov replied. "Perhaps you can be that for me?"

Seriously? Matthews thought. *Any idiot could incorporate his own business; it took about an hour and cost a hundred bucks. Maybe a little more.* Matthews wasn't exactly sure, never having served as the registered agent for a company.

"And put together some paperwork for me," the Russian continued.

Matthews hesitated, not because it sounded difficult, but because it involved paper. He preferred collecting clients' cash and running to court to plea bargain their cases. It was an easy living, if you could find the work.

"I will pay good money," Prolokov said. He leaned forward and looked directly into Matthews' eyes. "Fifty thousand dollars."

That might not be a lot of money in some legal circles, but it was a huge amount in Matthews' world. A $50,000 retainer was equivalent to two or maybe three months' gross income, depending on how Matthews maintained his accounting.

Sean Matthews had attended a second-tier law school at night over four years while holding down two part-time jobs, one as a janitor. When he graduated, no corporation or trade group hired him, probably because he was at the bottom of his class. He couldn't get a job with the federal government or on Capitol Hill. The local prosecutor's office never returned his call for an interview, and even the public defender wasn't interested.

Out of necessity, he hung a shingle, "Sean Matthews, Attorney at Law." The best thing that happened to him was the formation of a partnership with Mo Katz. But that didn't last, not after Katz had a whiff of how Matthews ran his operation.

"Is that not enough?" Prolokov sat back in the chair. "You need more? Seventy-five?" The Russian eyed the attorney shrewdly.

Matthews tried to sound casual. "I think I may be able to accommodate your need for counsel." Then he added, "Of course, I will need the entire retainer up front."

"The money is already in an account with arrangements for you to access it," Prolokov laughed. "You can withdraw as much as you want over whatever period of time you deem most advisable."

Prolokov found a pen on Matthews' desk and wrote down the name of a bank and a series of numbers on a piece of paper. "Here is the account information," he said. Then he reached into his coat pocket and removed a business card. "Here is how you can reach me." He placed the card on top of the paper and slid them across the desk.

Matthews picked up the card without carefully examining it. "I'll be back in touch in about two weeks," he said, tucking the card into one of the brochures provided by Prolokov. He put the paper with the numbers on it in his coat pocket. "I'm on vacation starting tomorrow. Going to a place called Columbia Bay. Are you familiar with it?" Prolokov shook his head. "Too bad," Matthews said. "It's a little piece of paradise. Nothing much ever happens there, which is why I like it."

**

Matthews awoke in the middle of the night. He felt a burning sensation in his chest. Stumbling out of bed, he went to the window and opened the blinds. He glanced across the room at the digital clock where 2:22 flashed in red digits. He looked outside. The sidewalk, apartment buildings and store fronts, street lights, and parked cars stood lifelessly in the dark night. A bead of sweat formed on his chest. He touched his T-shirt and felt sweat. He had perspired heavily.

Matthews sat on the windowsill and stared mindlessly into the night. He wondered whether he had been awakened by a bad dream. He tried to remember. One instant it seemed he could reconstruct the dream, the next instant it vanished.

He returned to bed but could not get back to sleep. An hour later, he got up, opened the sliding glass mirror to his closet, and retrieved the paper he had stuck into his coat pocket. He walked to his study and sat down at his desktop computer. Following the instructions on the paper, Matthews transferred $75,000.00 to his personal banking account.

CHAPTER 4

Prolokov searched madly but in vain. He had written down the names, but where? He looked in his shirt pocket, front and back trouser pockets, wallet, jacket, briefcase, desk, upstairs, downstairs, in the car. Nothing.

He even returned to the attorney's office, the one he had retained in order to try to gain inside information about Hutton's work on BOM. Still nothing.

Then he remembered.

Now, in the middle of the night, standing on a cracked sidewalk outside a bar and listing forward and back, he dialed the number stored in his phone, the one he was only permitted to call in an emergency.

The call was answered on the first ring.

Prolokov explained the situation. After enduring severe rebuke for ten minutes, Prolokov mentioned Columbia Bay. The words were greeted with silence. Then, the reedy voice on the other end asked, "What did you just say?"

"He is going on vacation at a place called Columbia Bay," Prolokov replied. "His girlfriend is already down there, the one who represents BOM."

Long, sustained laughter followed. "You have fallen into the schmaltz-grub, Boris. Yes, my friend, you've fallen into the schmaltz-grub." The man suddenly sounded pleased.

Prolokov smiled tentatively, unsure of what had just happened.

CHAPTER 5

Katz spent Saturday working on the BOM case in his office adjacent to the U.S. courthouse for the Eastern District of Virginia located in the Eisenhower Valley, a short distance from the Beltway and the Wilson Bridge.

Most of his deputies, assistant deputies and line attorneys were home with their families, enjoying the Labor Day holiday and lamenting the end of summer. The routine would resume on Tuesday with a steady stream of jury and non-jury trials in civil and criminal cases; an ongoing grand jury proceeding; meetings with witnesses, informants, law enforcement officers, and defense attorneys; and conferences with other U.S. Attorney offices.

He was understandably surprised when he was unexpectedly summoned to the large conference room at 2 in the afternoon.

He was greeted by a group of about 50 people who broke into applause as he walked into the room. Nearly half were in military uniforms. He recognized the group as the parents, children, wives and husbands, and sisters and brothers of the Marines who lost their lives as a result of Magellan's malfeasance. The room brimmed with emotion, some faces smiling and others holding back tears. A few staff members were also in the room.

"We just wanted to tell you we're damn proud of what your office is doing," hollered a man with a ruddy tan and a square jaw. Several let out a cheer. "You make proud the sons and daughters we've lost," the man added.

Katz realized it was a sort of pep rally, a gathering organized by the plaintiffs who demanded retribution from BOM. They were making a concerted effort to maintain high morale as the federal prosecutors pushed to settle the case or take it to trial.

Katz noticed Phil Landry standing in the back of the room. Landry's short, muscular legs, long torso and large skull were unmistakable. Landry, head of the antiterrorism office for the metropolitan area, raised a beefy hand in salute, a scowl across his face.

Although the gathering caught Katz off guard, he was prepared to address the group, having thought of little else other than the BOM case for months. He cleared his throat. "This case would never have been initiated without your unwavering faith and commitment," he said. "Your tenacity, the tenacity of every member of every family represented here today, enables us to push forward. We are going to prevail and bring this reprehensible institution to justice."

The room was suddenly silent; the cheering that greeted him over. Katz considered discussing the billions of dollars in civil penalties he hoped to obtain in settling the case, but decided against it. Intuitively, he understood they had not come here to listen to him talk about the money.

"Five years ago, a bomb struck a Humvee on a dusty street in Iraq. The militants who planted the roadside IED were trained in Libya. The militants' training was financed by the Bank of Magellan, which transferred billions of dollars from Fleet Street, Wall Street, Frankfurt, Beijing and Singapore to terrorist groups.

"Equipped with that knowledge, you, the people in this room, launched a class action lawsuit against Magellan. You wanted to hold them accountable for financing terrorism. As a result, Magellan met clandestinely with many of your families, offering attractive out-of-court settlements to stave off litigation. None of you accepted. You hung together. You all wanted the same thing, namely justice. And I think that moment is close at hand."

Suddenly one of the mothers called out from the back of the room. "We want a criminal conviction." Another hollered, "Charge the people behind this atrocity criminally."

Katz got it. This was not a pep rally at all. It was a lobbying effort organized to remind him and his staff that the plaintiffs desired a criminal conviction.

A young Marine stood. "My name is Richard Bellows," he said. "My kid brother died in that attack while attempting to save the lives of his fellow Marines. My parents and I are proud that he performed such an honorable act, putting the life of others ahead of his own." He looked over at his mom and dad. "We're not satisfied with a money settlement, Mr. Katz. If that's all we wanted, we could have done it by ourselves. We want a criminal conviction."

As he listened, Katz mentally reviewed the factors in a ten-year-old Justice Department memorandum penned by former Attorney General Eric Holder concerning criminal charges against corporations. The factors included the seriousness of the offense, the pervasiveness of the wrongdoing, the corporation's history of similar conduct, and the voluntary disclosure of the wrongdoing.

In the BOM case, all of those factors pointed toward criminal indictment. Marines had died. BOM had laundered terrorist monies for years. And it had hidden its wrongdoing while seeking to settle cases without disclosing facts or permitting affected parties to collaborate with one another.

Despite the recent decline in prosecutions of corporate wrongdoers, Katz knew it could be done. After all, BP had pled guilty to 11 counts of felony manslaughter in connection with the Deepwater Horizon explosion, in addition to the $1.25 billion the oil company paid in criminal damages. Tokyo-based Takata Corp. pled guilty to one count for wire fraud and paid $1 billion in criminal penalties. And Volkswagen pled to three criminal felonies related to its emissions scandal.

"I'll work on it," Katz said. "It's always been under consideration. We're trying to build a criminal case. If we can build a strong enough case, I'll pursue it. I promise you."

The group broke out in a cheer.

As the impromptu meeting adjourned, the young Marine who had spoken approached Katz. He produced a group of photos: his slain brother with his wife and a daughter around five years old. He held each picture reverently. The photos showed a young family hopeful and aspirational, expecting a future that would never come to fruition. A tear fell on one of the photos. The Marine touched it, trying to absorb the tear from his eye into his thumb.

It did not absorb. It smudged. Katz watched the Marine tremble as he tried to get his emotions under control.

"I'm so sorry for your loss," Katz said. "How is she doing, his wife? What about the little girl?"

Bellows cleared his throat. "We don't know. We've lost contact. Cindy couldn't handle the pain. She's somewhere out West, maybe northern California, Sonoma County, we think." He choked back more tears. "This is the only grandchild my parents have and they never see her. All they can do is think about her, and worry, and hope that the pain lessens enough for the family to get back together someday."

The Marine looked at Katz. His eyes were pockets of water. "These men are merchants of death, Mr. Katz. They might just as well have planted the IED that killed my brother. You have to punish them.

"Don't be complacent. Don't be satisfied with a civil settlement. The bank doesn't bleed or cry. Something more is needed. Someone's responsible for this, probably someone smart enough to evade the law and hide behind a corporate name, avoiding responsibility and liability. Prosecute them criminally."

"I'll see what I can do," Katz promised. "I promise you."

The Marine smiled. "They say you're the best in the business, that you find a way with the law. Everyone is counting on you, Mr. Katz."

**

After the event ended, Katz ran into Landry as he entered the men's room.

"Didn't expect to see you here, Phil," Katz said.

Landry did not answer. He simply scowled.

"Something the matter?" asked Katz.

"Yes," Landry replied. "You're the matter."

While the encounter was unexpected, Landry's attitude was not a surprise. The leader of the antiterrorism task force harbored an animus toward Katz that defied credulity. Katz could not understand why the rules of common civility did not apply even in the most casual encounters.

The hostility boiled over instantly. "You should not be in this office," Landry said pointedly. "You're an accidental prosecutor, and here you are telling stories about truth, justice, and the American way. Let's be honest. You've spent most of your professional life obfuscating the law and bending the rules."

Katz hesitated before he said, "You really need to get over the past, Phil."

"You really aren't cut out for being U.S. Attorney," Landry said, pushing his way past Katz and into the hall.

CHAPTER 6

Late in the afternoon, Katz called together several members of his staff who remained in the office, including Mai Lin and Mike "Mac" McCarthy.

Lin, a talented research assistant in her mid-20s, accompanied Katz to the U.S. Attorney's office after helping crack the Daingerfield Island case. Her cherubic smile, warm eyes, and easy manner had a calming influence in the office. Lin steered the direction of major criminal and civil cases with an uncanny ability to anticipate problems and find solutions to thorny legal issues.

McCarthy headed the BOM team. He was in his late 30s, with wavy red hair, sharp eyes, and strong Irish features. Mac was arrogant, but others overlooked it due to his prodigious work output and impressive record of convictions.

He was a former legislative staff director to Senator Abraham Lowenstein, chairman of the Senate Intelligence Committee. Lowenstein championed Katz's selection as U.S. Attorney and had asked Katz to hire his staff director in a senior position. Katz obliged by naming McCarthy deputy of the criminal division.

"You must have sensed my apprehension in addressing those folks earlier today," Katz confided. His tone was somber, but not angry. "I don't know who engineered today's get-together, but it certainly had its desired effect. If I was straddling the fence about whether to seek criminal charges against BOM, today's little demonstration settled the matter."

No one admitted organizing the meeting, but a few eyes darted in Lin's direction. Detecting their movement, Katz said to Lin, "Thank you for everything you do for this office." Then, to the group, he added: "We are going to build as strong a criminal case as possible against BOM. Once we've got all of the elements covered to secure a conviction, we'll include a criminal count as part of a proposed plea agreement. Understood?"

Everyone nodded in agreement.

McCarthy said, "We've got a conference planned for the 12th with Jane Hutton, BOM's counsel."

"Then you don't have a minute to spare," Katz said. He did not share that Hutton was vacationing at Columbia Bay. Hopefully, her side would be less prepared than their side.

As they were wrapping up, Katz asked, "Say, who invited Phil Landry?"

No one took responsibility.

Katz asked no further questions. He remained unsettled by his encounter with Landry, who was aggrieved over something. Katz was curious to know what it was, and why Landry was in attendance in the first place. He was not a common face around the office and had only rendered assistance in the early stages of the BOM inquiry. Something was up.

**

Shortly before midnight, a fisherman steered an aluminum boat along the eastern shore of the Potomac River off Rosalie Island opposite Jones Point. The inlet was a prize fishing hole but tonight nothing was biting.

He turned the boat west and headed out north of the Wilson Bridge. He navigated to one of the bridge's pylons partially hidden by a massive canvas sheet that hung from the highway and pedestrian walkway to the water. The word PASHA was displayed across the sheet.

As the fisherman approached the pylon, the canvas tarp snapped back. The unexpected movement spooked him, and he momentarily lost his balance, nearly falling off the boat into the water. The tarp continued flapping in the wind as gusts swept across the river and around the pylon.

In the distance, the Ferris wheel spun slowly at the edge of National Harbor, its kaleidoscopic colors enhancing the Maryland shore. Overhead, the fisherman heard the steady whir of traffic rolling across the Wilson Bridge. To his left and right, the dark waters of the river swirled around him.

His curiosity led him to investigate what was behind the tarp. As he came closer, the canvas flapped again like an elephant's ear. Behind the tarp and beneath the bridge, he observed a floating platform filled with large wooden crates. The fisherman maneuvered the small boat alongside the platform. The boat rocked as he stepped out of it. He secured the vessel to the side of the platform and left it bobbing in the water.

The fisherman pulled a tiny flashlight out of his pocket. Its beam penetrated the dark like a laser. Insects quickly flew into its light like tiny actors seeking to audition.

Large wooden boxes were stacked on three sides of the platform, some of them covered with blue and brown tarps. The fisherman returned to his boat, pulled a plastic pouch from under the aluminum seat, and removed a screwdriver. He returned to the platform, balanced the flashlight between his jaw and collarbone, and pushed the screwdriver under the lid of one of the wood boxes, forcing it open.

As he did so, a bullet whizzed by the hand holding the screwdriver. At first, he assumed it was a bug or a piece of dirt. But then the second struck his arm, piercing skin and shattering bone. The fisherman screamed, but his voice was drowned out by the bridge traffic and the wind.

Four more bullets ripped through his torso in rapid succession. The screwdriver dropped from the fisherman's hand, hitting the lid of the wooden box. The flashlight struck the platform. The tarp flew open. The fisherman saw his boat bobbing in the water and tried to move toward it. He dropped to his knees as he took the first step. His body fell face down onto the wooden platform.

A hand reached down and turned off the flashlight.

CHAPTER 7

Midday Sunday, September 1, Matthews buckled his seatbelt and prepared for takeoff from Reagan National Airport. He ran a hand over his unkempt hair, sat back, and closed his drooping eyes. He had barely slept a wink since waking up Friday night.

The rubber wheels of the airplane moved down the runway, gaining speed, bumping along the tarmac. The plane's body vibrated slightly. Then liftoff, wheels tucking into the belly of the fuselage with a thump.

He sensed the wonderful feeling of being airborne, like being seated on a carnival ride. He was leaving everything behind on the ground, unfinished, temporarily forgotten. His body, mind, and spirit wandered aimlessly, almost weightlessly, freed from earthly moorings.

Matthews looked out the window to where the water splashed against the banks of the Potomac River. His eyes fell on a barge laboring upriver and a speedboat racing toward it. Pirates on the high seas of the Potomac, Matthews laughed to himself. He closed his eyes again as the plane veered slightly to the left.

Jane Hutton had already rented a car and driven to the village of Columbia Bay, situated midpoint between Charleston and Savannah. She was thinking of retiring in Columbia Bay someday. Matthews doubted she would.

Matthews' eyelids were blankets shielding his eyes and mind from thoughts about work. The weight of his job evaporated and, with it, the arguing, cajoling, pleading, praying, advocating, enticing, negotiating, and threatening that comprised his workday.

His encounter with Katz Friday night reminded him that the past decade of his life had been spent in the bowels of the criminal justice system, plying a trade built on petty misdemeanants and drunk drivers. Any deadbeat, loser, sap, druggie, miscreant or unlucky bastard found a welcome sign on the mat outside his office. His practice was very different from Hutton's highbrow clientele. She had moved straight from the bar exam into the D.C. branch of a New York firm that dealt with corporate clients. Truth be told, though, she simply represented a higher class of miscreant, a better-paying one.

The silver jet glided through the blue afternoon sky, which was punctuated by puffs of clouds that looked like they were made of cotton candy and bubbles. Music played in the background. Did it come from the headphones of the person seated next to him or was it in his head? Something classical. And that whirring sound. Was that the air flow overhead or the roar of the jet engines outside the window, under the wing?

Matthews pulled a tri-fold pamphlet in heavy expensive paper out of his carry-on bag. It bore the logo and name of Pasha Construction across its cover. Colorful illustrations of roads, bridges, and overpasses were interspersed with minimal text.

Pasha was not diversified like Shaw Construction Corp. or ubiquitous like Bechtel. In the Washington market, it was not a name associated with residential, commercial, engineering and transportation projects. Its banner did not fly on cranes adjacent to rising residential complexes or on the chain-link fences surrounding construction sites.

The only place one could see its name was on a huge banner that hung over the side of the Wilson Bridge, dangling from the roadbed nearly down to the water and covering an entire link of the bridge.

Matthews removed Prolokov's business card from the pamphlet. The front read:

Boris Prolokov, President
Pasha Construction Co.

Oddly, there was a telephone number but no address. Matthews flipped the card over. Several words were scribbled in cursive on the back. Matthews recited the first word out loud. "Gadfly." He studied the word before recalling a line from Plato's Apology of the life of Socrates.

I am the gadfly of the Athenian people, given to them by God, and they will never have another, if they kill me.

Matthews slid the card into his wallet and returned the pamphlet to his carry-on, then leaned back in the seat and dozed. Again, he heard music. In his mind, the flight attendant, dressed in a red outfit with gold piping and a hat with a chin strap, played a viola.

When the plane touched down in Charleston, Matthews awoke, wonderfully restored for the first time in two days. He smiled at the thought of everything going his way.

**

While Matthews was settling in his seat for the trip to Columbia Bay, a heavily laden barge wended its way up the Potomac River. The pusher boat that was herding its bulk upriver looked like a tugboat on steroids, with its square nose, shallow draft and white wooden superstructure. Its pilot was invisible in the cockpit, but four crewmen perched atop the crates on the barge itself.

The barge moved slowly. One of the crewmen, bored with the pace, began singing a tune written by John Fogerty of Creedence Clearwater Revival and covered by Ike and Tina Turner: *Proud Mary*, with its refrain *rollin' on the river.* The others joined in.

Like a small train, the paired vessels passed the Occoquan Basin and the Mount Vernon mansion standing on a bluff, its bright white porch and red roof announcing antebellum aristocracy.

The barge's freight had reportedly arrived from Hamburg or Amsterdam; no one was really sure of the point of origin. There had been some confusion about that in Tidewater. Some said it had originally landed in Charleston and been carried north to Hampton Roads. Some of the material was for a construction company doing repair work on the Wilson Bridge span, too bulky or heavy or hazardous to be carried by truck or train to northern Virginia. The remainder of the freight was headed up the Potomac River, toward the Washington Channel and the rebuilding of the Southwest waterfront. Or so they said.

An elongated speedboat suddenly appeared from around Jones Point, whose acre of parkland lay at the confluence of Hunting Creek and the Potomac River. The speedboat arrowed out into the placid river, leaving a frothy wake.

The chugging of the pusher boat's engine changed cadence as it idled in deep water. The intercepting vessel came starboard and slowed so the boats could link up as a replacement crew from the speedboat stepped onboard the pusher boat. With the exception of the captain, the bargemen who had traveled upriver transferred into the speedboat. Wads of money changed hands, and the bargemen grinned in appreciation.

With a wave from the captain, the speedboat raced away. The barge resumed its journey up the Potomac, slowly heading beneath the span of the Wilson Bridge. The speedboat raced to a dock along the Alexandria waterfront where the crew disembarked and walked lazily up King Street, no one asking any questions.

CHAPTER 8

The Washington, D.C., area was a ghost town on Labor Day. Streets were deserted and stores stood empty. Shops once filled with frantic parents and students searching for school supplies and clothes were uninhabited, the victims of online shopping. Teens lingered at pools preparing to close for the season; families cluttered the highways in their SUVs returning from vacations; and everyone else found their way to some event to bid farewell to summer.

Around noon, a text message appeared on Landry's phone. He glanced at it as he stood in the deserted lobby of the Crystal City office building that housed the antiterrorism task force. It read:

CRATES HERE; STORED SAME PLACE AS OTHERS.
NEED TO TRANSFER SOONEST.

Landry reread the text and ran calculations in his head. The crates could be transferred to the warehouse later this week. If the final delivery arrived the following Friday, then it could be transferred on September 17, Constitution Day.

A look of satisfaction crossed his face. The operation he had guided for the past year was on the verge of success. In about two weeks, he would be hailed a hero for saving the city from the throes of evil terrorists.

A few details needed tending, like ensuring BOM was settled expeditiously, so as to remove any possibility that a certain person of interest would be identified and charged in the case. But tying up loose ends came with the territory. The important thing was that the major pieces were in place. He had everything under control. From this point forward, it was only a matter of time.

Landry's thumbs worked the keyboard on his personal phone. The middle of the night was always the best time because it caused the least inconvenience and raised the fewest suspicions, he reasoned. So far, the state authorities regulating the bridge had been accommodating and had not asked too many questions. He texted his response.

PICK UP 1:30 AM THURS, SEPT. 5.
FINAL DELIVERY NEXT FRIDAY.

Landry sighed. Being a handler was no fun. He wished he was young again, back in the fray, instead of barking instructions from the sidelines and hoping less experienced underlings did as they were told.

Landry departed the building and got into his car parked on Clark Street. He revved the engine and hugged the curb as the car roared south through Crystal City. He executed a sharp U-turn and shot up the 45-degree ramp that fed onto the airport access road to Reagan National Airport. He maneuvered through the twists and turns around the airport and spilled onto the southbound lanes of the George Washington Parkway to Alexandria.

He rubbed his hand over his forehead and temples like a washcloth as he headed into Old Town. His mind continued to run through a series of scenarios, looking for signs of potential trouble.

Tomorrow he would call Senator Lowenstein's office to arrange a meeting for Thursday morning. Over the past decades, their careers had crossed paths like vines on a lattice. They needed one another to survive in Washington, where intelligence information was passed in exchange for political cover. Together, they spun stories, leaked classified information, and destroyed enemies. He needed to keep Lowenstein informed, at least peripherally, if for no other reason than to provide some cover for himself.

CHAPTER 9

"Did you pack a dinner jacket?" Hutton asked, pushing crisp salad greens into her mouth. It was the day after Labor Day and everyone had left Columbia Bay for points inland. Tonight they were out for a late dinner after spending a long afternoon strolling through town, visiting art galleries, eating ice cream, and touring the bay.

Dinner jacket? Did he look like a man who packed formal togs for vacation? "No," he replied. "I brought some polo shirts. I'm not planning on any formal functions."

"You're going to the club in cutoffs?"

"I'm staying as far from that crowd as possible."

"Would bringing a suit and tie really create such an imposition?"

"I don't — "

"— think it's anyone's business what you do on your vacation. It's your time to relax and the hell with anyone's rules."

Matthews didn't hide his irritation. She always did that, finished sentences for him after asking questions to which she knew the answers, or at least thought she did. It drove him crazy.

"I just wanted to see if you're excited about this trip," she replied. Sometimes she came across as too much of a high-powered corporate counsel type, which also grated on him, she knew.

"I'm never excited about trips that revolve around meeting the same people day in and day out," he said.

Hutton had bright red wavy hair that swept down along the sides of her face and rested luxuriously on her shoulders. Her eyes twinkled like sapphires in a delicate yet steely freckled face. She had an impossibly elongated neck, white and smooth as a Greek statue's. She was as tall as Matthews, perhaps an inch or two taller, five foot ten or eleven, with long arms and legs. Appearance was important to her: She had packed for every conceivable occasion, even unpacked and started over several times. It might be rainy out on the island this time of year, or they might end up encountering a cold front. She didn't want to get caught unprepared.

Their vacation on Columbia Bay was supposed to last through next Monday. Senior members of her large firm were scheduled to join them this weekend. The junior attorneys would remain back at the office, working assiduously on the BOM case.

Hutton was not worried about being adequately prepared for an upcoming conference with the U.S. Attorney's office. She knew the case inside and out. More important, she had read up on her adversary, Mike McCarthy, and regarded him as weak and ineffectual in a hard negotiation. After all, he was a product of Capitol Hill, where outsiders cowered in deference to members of Congress and their senior staff without ever testing their mettle. She knew McCarthy got his job because of his political connections and not because of any demonstrated legal prowess. Next week, she would teach him a thing or two about the real world.

She would succeed in the BOM case like she succeeded in everything else, except having a lasting intimate relationship, which was the reason a loser like Matthews was in her life.

"Are you listening?"

Hutton looked up at Matthews.

"I said I'm never excited about trips we take to hook up with the same people you see day in and day out."

She knew how he felt, but it wasn't a matter of boredom and avoiding routine. She had a theory that he was apprehensive because her former boyfriend from the firm would be there. He always acted weird around her exes. This had been evidenced on multiple occasions.

"You're just a spoilsport," she replied, not wanting to go there.

They finished dinner. The waiter asked if either wanted another glass of wine. Both said yes. The wine filled the space created by their silence.

"How do you want to pay?" Hutton asked when it was finally time to leave.

"Cash," he answered.

"No," she said. "That's not what I mean. Do you want to split the bill?"

What a stupid thing to ask, he thought. *Since when did they split bills? Unbelievable. What next? Sleep in separate rooms when they returned to their cottage? Or maybe call it a night right here in tiny*

Columbia Bay? He could take a cab and rent a room at a cheap hotel out on the interstate.

"Sure," he said.

She laughed. "You said that just to irritate me. Didn't you?"

"Sure," he repeated.

She laughed again.

**

The waiter arrived with the bill. Matthews pulled a fat wad of cash out of his back pocket, glancing at the bar opposite them as he did so. There were a couple of guys there, staring into their drinks.

"Where did you get *that*?" Hutton asked, lowering her voice.

Matthews seldom carried cash. No one did. If Washington, Lincoln, Jackson, and Grant lined up on one side of the room, few people would be able to match the correct president with the proper denomination, except for Washington and Lincoln, maybe.

"You *always* use credit," Hutton continued. Actually, the truth was that she normally paid, but there was no advantage to reminding him of that now. "Seriously, Sean. Where did that come from?"

The truth? A client paid a retainer in cash from penny-ante drug sales. Matthews had stuffed the money in his pocket last Friday night when he returned to the office from the Lyceum. It saved him running to an ATM to access his new wealth from Prolokov. What was he supposed to tell her?

"No, don't tell me," she said, half answering her own question. She knew all about his practice and suspected it was drug money. She also suspected the cash portion of the retainer would be off the books to avoid paying taxes. He had low overhead, low-class clients, and a low rating with the state bar.

"My tenant paid cash," Matthews lied, referring to the junkie who occupied an unkempt hole in the basement below his law office, a hovel replete with county code violations but reliable for covering a portion of his mortgage payment. "He must have won a poker game. He's always late with the rent, but this time he paid up his back rent plus next month's." Matthews laughed the sort of laugh intended to end a discussion.

"How much have you got on you?" Hutton couldn't resist asking. She acted like he was carrying a loaded gun.

"Three grand." Matthews peeled off a few bills and put them on the table, then stuffed the remainder in his pocket.

"It looks like a lot more than that."

"When was the last time you saw three thousand dollars in cash?" he asked sarcastically.

The waiter scooped up the cash with the check. He looked at Matthews, who gave him a nod to keep the change. "Thanks, sir," he said happily, a young kid with a mop of fair hair and a goofy grin.

Hutton and Matthews got up and walked out into the night.

A smudge of moon was veiled behind thin wisps of cloud. No stars were discernible. The streets were bathed in blackness, as were the spaces between buildings.

An eerie presence engulfed them. It had departed the restaurant with them, like a gust of air sweeping out the door and clinging to their clothing. Although neither turned, they both felt the presence behind them.

At first, it was only a sense. Then they heard footsteps keeping pace with their own.

Matthews swept Hutton to the left at the end of the street toward their car parked a block away. The street was empty. Hutton casually glanced behind and saw a male figure in the shadows. She took Matthews by the arm and leaned into him.

He walked her off the sidewalk and into the middle of the street, attempting to get away from the shadows. He pulled his free hand out of his pants pocket and dropped it to his side, forming a fist.

"Sean," said the voice behind them. "Jane." Their names were spoken flatly, lifelessly, in a menacing tone. "Don't turn around again. If you do, I'll shoot you."

**

Three hours later, Katz's phone rang, rousing him from a sound sleep. He rolled over, picked up the phone, and glanced at the screen, which read "Sean Matthews." Katz put down the phone, punched the pillow, found his space on the mattress, checked to see whether Snowe had been disturbed, and, seeing her resting comfortably, resumed a peaceful night's sleep.

Elsewhere, a call was placed to Prolokov. The Russian awoke, startled. He reached for his phone, illuminated in the dark. The ringing stopped. He studied the number on the screen. He did not recognize the number, but surmised the reason for the call. He dialed it.

"I have a bit of a situation," the voice on the other end said nervously.

CHAPTER 10

Early Wednesday morning, Katz and Snowe found one another among the sheets of their king-size bed. He performed his usual ritual before they made love, lighting three candles and arranging them on each bedside table and the bureau so as to form a triangle of glowing light around the bed. Things had to be just so. She rolled her eyes as he went through his routine.

By the time they were ready for a shower, the bed had found its way two feet from the wall and the sheets spilled onto the bedroom floor in all directions like discarded clothes. The candles had burned down a good amount as well.

After they showered, he made breakfast, pouring cereal and almond milk into bowls. He made strong coffee and brought in the newspaper, which had been thrown on the porch and lodged in one of the wicker chairs like a ball in a mitt.

"I may have to leave for a few days," Snowe said reluctantly as they sat engrossed in the coffee and papers. "My sisters need a break. It's my turn to care for Mom."

"Take all the time you need."

"Are you going to be okay if it's a week or two?"

He gave her a sly look, wondering if this was why their lovemaking had not waited until the weekend. She read his mind. They both laughed. "I'll manage," he said, adding, "I'll be surprised if I do anything other than work long hours on the BOM."

**

In his office late in the afternoon, Katz pressed the speaker on his desk phone and called his special assistant, Curtis Santana, whose skills as a private investigator were unrivaled. Like Lin and McCarthy, Santana had moved to the U.S. Attorney's office with Katz, who preferred to surround himself with loyal subordinates rather than career public servants. While Santana pretended to be satisfied with his new position, he missed the hustlers he routinely surveilled when he ran his own shop.

Santana took the call near Middleburg, where he was driving along the Virginia countryside in an old Fiat Spider. Leaves showed only the earliest signs of autumn. None had yet fallen. The landscape was green and brown, with hay baled at the edges of fields like huge rolls of print paper. The sky was a rich blue, and the air sweeping through the small convertible was warm, with an occasional ribbon of cool air in the mix.

"I had an unexpected guest attend Monday's meeting with the families of the dead Marines," Katz said. "Phil Landry was in the back of the room."

Santana pulled up the collar of his leather jacket and looked in the rear-view mirror, then downshifted at a hairpin turn. "I don't necessarily see it as all that unusual," he said into the Bluetooth system, with both his hands held firmly on the leather steering wheel. Strands of hair flew in front of his sunglasses, and he brushed them back. "Maybe he sees a role for the task force in the BOM case. That wouldn't be unusual."

"He hasn't offered any assistance since the early stages of our inquiry," Katz replied. "No, I think he was there to keep tabs on our progress, although I have no explanation as to why he cares."

Santana came to an intersection with stop signs at every corner. He came to a stop, downshifted into first gear, and swept his eyes to the other three corners. Then he pressed the accelerator pedal and raced ahead.

"So what's this got to do with me?" Santana asked.

"I want you to follow him and see what he's up to."

Santana laughed. "Be serious, Mo. I'm not going to tail the head of the D.C. area's antiterrorism task force. I know there's bad blood between you two, but this isn't something that warrants surveillance."

Katz scratched his chin. He'd forgotten to shave. He pushed back his chair and eased his loafers up onto the edge of his desk. "I don't know, Curtis, but something is not right."

"The man's doing his job, just like the rest of us."

"Okay," Katz said. "But if he shows up unexpectedly one more time, I'm going to ask you to pay a visit to his headquarters in Crystal City and do a little sleuthing."

"Fair enough," Santana said, signing off before taking a gentle curve in the road at an accelerated rate of speed.

As Katz ended the call, he saw Lin standing in the doorway. She had one foot inside his office and the other in the hallway, as if uncertain whether to enter or retreat.

"What's up?" he asked.

"I just dropped by to thank you for your kind words on Saturday," she said, pretending not to have overheard the conversation with Santana. "I appreciate your compliment, but I'm really the one who should be thanking you for giving me this incredible opportunity. I love working in this office."

He knew she did. "How's David doing?" he asked, inquiring about David Reese, her fiancé. Reese was in his second year of law school and was about to begin an internship with the Alexandria Police. Katz had arranged for Reese to work for Stone.

"He's doing great. The internship dovetails with his interest in the criminal justice system," she replied. "And Ms. Stone will be a wonderful mentor. I'll tell David you asked about him."

As she started to walk away, Lin hesitated as she processed the conversation between Katz and Santana. She wished Santana was more willing to figure out if Landry was up to something nefarious. Like Katz, she was suspicious and wondered whether she should say something.

"Is everything okay?" Katz asked.

"Yes, of course," she replied quickly. Then she asked, "If we invited you to dinner, would you come? Would you bring Abby?"

"Abby's going out of town to be with her mom," Katz said, taken aback. "But, yes, I'd love an invitation to dinner some night. If nothing else, it'll save me having to order carryout."

Lin replied, "Not necessarily. I wasn't suggesting that either David or I would be cooking. We'll just be ordering carryout for three, that's all."

Katz smiled. They were a beautiful couple, both engaged in things they loved. He hoped the future was kind to them.

**

Santana slowed the car to a crawl as he approached another four-way stop sign. He shifted into first. He might have convinced the boss, but the conversation with Katz had left him uneasy. Santana had been suspicious of Landry since spring, around the time the task force moved to Crystal City. Landry had sequestered himself in an office with a small cadre of task force members who rarely mingled with other federal, state, or local law enforcement agencies. They held their cards close, too close, so far as Santana was concerned.

Pressing his foot to the accelerator, Santana shot across the intersection and shifted the car through the gears, roaring along a roadway paralleling two white fences demarcating pastoral acreage. A few bales of hay were already stacked in a field near a tidy farmhouse. A dog raced down a gravel driveway, greeting the approaching speedster with unwelcoming barks. The sun moved down the tree line.

Santana placed a call. Fortunately, there was no answer and he was able to just leave a message. "Hey, babe," he said. "The good news is I'm heading back, but the bad news is I won't be dropping over to your place. Something's come up."

As he hung up the phone, Santana looked at the evening sky. Blue was turning to purple. Dusk approached.

CHAPTER 11

Crystal City's landscape was sculpted with a few grand, sweeping architectural gems and a lot of cement and glass cubes, as high as they were wide, with tired façades. An array of one-way streets wound about the eclectic edifices, creating a jumbled pathway through the urban dysfunction.

Landry sat in a large interior conference room on the 9th floor of one of the cement cubes. It was nearly 9 p.m. The room was dark except for a single light that shone on a model of a bridge displayed in the center of a 30-seat table extending the length of the room.

As he stared at the model, Landry thought back to last September when he discovered illegal transactions by a person of interest in the BOM investigation. Recognizing that Landry had uncovered his misdeeds, the person of interest offered an enticing proposition. If Landry ceased his investigation, the person of interest promised to provide him with details of another major criminal operation.

The person of interest claimed to know a renegade group of foreign and domestic extremists who wanted to get their hands on heavy-duty military grade munitions, including outlawed surface-to-air missiles.

Landry doubted the assertion was true. More likely, he thought, the person of interest would plant the idea in the mind of some imprudent malcontent. It was a pattern repeated time and again by criminals to win favor with the law. Landry likened it to the drug dealer who provided contraband to a mule and then claimed the drug courier was his distributor. The poor sap got charged with possession to distribute while the kingpin walked away free and clear.

It was a gross miscarriage of justice, but an effective way to stage a bust. Landry had no problem with that. Plus, his plan had star appeal. He could set up a phony scheme to ship surface-to-air missiles to the D.C. area. The missiles would be dummies to ensure no one was injured, except maybe for the last shipment, when Landry might substitute the real thing for special effect. It was guaranteed to make a splash on the front page of *The Washington Post* and make Landry a superstar in the law enforcement community.

Landry even had the perfect location, namely the Wilson Bridge. He recalled an incident in 2018 when a tractor-trailer collided with a boom truck on the bridge, leaving one person dead and several injured. People familiar with the incident viewed it as a tragedy, but not Landry, who saw the bridge as a steel trap that could be used to corner and arrest the extremists.

Under the auspices of the person of interest, a crew of 14 men was assembled. The four core members were Russian, all of whom possessed some military training. The remainder were malcontents, ingrates, mercenaries, and grifters. Everyone was motivated by money, large amounts of which were promised to secure their participation.

Landry was so consumed in his thoughts about the operation that he did not hear the sound of the elevator door as it opened or the footsteps approaching the conference room.

**

A few minutes earlier, Lin had stood at the entrance of the building looking for a way to get inside. Two sets of doors leading to an ornate glass and marble lobby were locked. She called building management from the outside line, but was told access was restricted.

Fortunately, after she hung up the phone, the elevator doors opened and a man walked absentmindedly across the lobby. As he opened the front door, she approached and flashed her U.S. Attorney's badge dangling on the lanyard around her neck. He held the door for her and she glided inside. "Don't work too late," he said with a wry smile.

"I'm only picking up some material and then I'm gone," she said. "Have a great rest of the night."

Once inside the elevator, she pushed the button for the 9th floor, knowing the antiterrorism task force was headquartered on that floor. The door closed but the elevator did not budge. Then the door opened. The elevator was like a rocket without a booster; it wasn't going anywhere unless she had an access card to a specific floor.

Undeterred, Lin tried again, with the same result. Then a third and fourth time. Finally, she exited the elevator and found a stairwell, which was locked. She walked to the far end of the lobby and boarded the freight elevator. She pressed the button for the 9th floor. The doors closed but the elevator remained motionless. Then she tried the top floor and the elevator responded, going up to 12.

Lin found a custodian vacuuming the hall and talked him into taking her down to the 9th floor. He obliged.

**

Lin looked through an opening in the screen that covered the glass wall separating the conference room from the hallway and served as a shield preventing passers-by from seeing inside the room.

She saw the bridge model glowing in an otherwise black, cavernous room. The model appeared both beautifully elegant and strangely ominous, its double-leaf bascule design spread across the table resembling seagulls in flight, the tips of their outspread wings touching one another. Although she did not know it, the model was an exact replica of the ten-lane drawbridge and represented to scale the 155-foot drawspan that made the Wilson Bridge one of the largest drawbridges in the world.

Lin did not see Landry, who was seated in the shadows with his back to the wall. She walked toward one of the two doors on either side of the glass wall leading to the conference room and turned the door handle. The sudden click jarred Landry, who swiveled around in his chair.

"Mai," he said as he recognized her. "What are you doing? How did you get in here?"

CHAPTER 12

Lin stepped inside the room. "What are *you* doing here?" she asked pointedly.

"No, seriously," Landry replied angrily. "How did you get in here? This is a restricted area."

She held his stare. "I'm picking up some files for Mr. McCarthy. Our office uses storage space on one of the floors, but I forgot which one. I've been wandering around trying to get my bearings."

He studied her quizzically. "Research documents are maintained on seven," he said. "You should try there, but I doubt anyone is in at this time of night. Didn't you think of that before you drove over?"

"It's related to the BOM case," she replied. "We're working round the clock. I was hoping someone would be here." She looked around. "At least I'm in the right building," she laughed.

Then her eyes returned to the model of the bridge in the center of the conference table, glowing under the single light illuminating the room. "What's this?" she asked.

Landry hesitated. "It's a model of the Wilson Bridge," he said. Then he added, "There's going to be a celebration on the bridge on Constitution Day."

"What kind of celebration? And what's Constitution Day? I'm not that familiar with it." The words tumbled out of her mouth. She tried to come across as ignorant, as a first-generation American whose parents had emigrated from Vietnam and who didn't understand a lot about American history. "Sorry if I'm asking stupid questions."

"Perfectly okay," Landry laughed. "It's not as popular as the Fourth of July, but arguably more important." His voice took on a professorial tone. "It's the day Congress adopted the Constitution, September 17th, 1787. The date September 17 is the same day they fought the Battle of Antietam during the Civil War." He paused, then added, "One generation created our country and, 75 years later, another generation preserved it."

Lin smiled. "You know a lot about history," she said. "Thanks for the lesson."

"Happy to oblige. It's a battle we continue to wage today against those who would do us harm."

Lin kept her gaze on the model. She thought Landry was a complete imbecile for being so easily fooled. Perhaps not everyone knew about Constitution Day, but she did, having been a history major in college. She'd read Thomas Paine's *Common Sense* and *The Federalist Papers,* and she doubted whether Landry had read either one. "But what's the story with the bridge?" she asked.

He got up. "There will be tall ships arriving in Washington on the 17th to celebrate Constitution Day. They'll stop at Mount Vernon first and then sail up the Potomac inside the Beltway to Old Town Alexandria and the D.C. wharf."

He grabbed a metal pointer that leaned against the wall and pointed the staff at the center of the bridge. "They're going to raise the drawbridge for the tall ships. My task force is coordinating with other law enforcement and antiterrorism groups to guard against any terrorist acts associated with the celebration."

Lin stepped further inside the room. As she did, she saw Landry stiffen. He realized she was intruding upon his private domain. Undeterred, she probed further. "That's so weird, having a drawbridge on an interstate highway, isn't it?" she asked innocently. "It must create havoc every time they raise that thing."

"The drawbridge is raised selectively," Landry answered in his professorial tone. "It's raised about 40 times a year, half of those for maintenance."

"Do they raise it often for tall ships?"

"They did just a couple of months ago, when the Tall Ship Providence visited Alexandria back on the Fourth of July," Landry answered.

"Which ships are coming this month?"

"I don't know their names. I think there's a replica of the USS Constitution and its sister ship the USS Constellation, but I'm not up on those details. I'm focused mostly on the bridge security."

As Lin stepped further inside the room, Landry began to feel threatened. He stepped back, placing the pointer at his side like a musket.

"Is this going to be a big deal, the Constitution Day celebration at the bridge?"

"Yes, it's a very big deal. They're going to shut down the interstate highway in the middle of a Tuesday afternoon, if that answers your question. We're going to fly a couple of helicopters onto the bridge and there'll be fire boats and other vessels in the vicinity to welcome the tall ships."

Landry stopped there. He had already shared too much information. He needed her to quit asking questions and to leave now.

"I haven't heard anything about this celebration," she said. "I'm spending too much time at the office. I'm going to read up on this when I get home tonight."

"There's not much information available yet. There's concern about security. All that traffic stopped on the interstate creates a soft target for terrorists, so we're not advertising the event until next Sunday, the 15th."

"I see," she said. "I'll keep a lookout for upcoming events."

**

Ten minutes later, Lin hurried outside. An autumn breeze raced down Clark Street, catching her black hair and tossing it in all directions. She took an elastic from her pocket and pulled her hair back into a ponytail.

Half a block away, Curtis Santana watched her pass beneath a street light heading to her car. He knew no one had access to the building she had exited unless they were cleared by the task force. Therefore, he concluded, Landry must have provided Lin with entry as part of a prearranged meeting.

Santana suspected someone might be leaking details about the BOM case. That would explain Landry's appearance on Monday. Until this instant, however, Lin was the last person he would have suspected to be collaborating with Landry. *And over what?* he asked himself.

As Lin sped away, Santana had a split second to decide whether to follow her or to wait for Landry. Most likely, he reasoned, Lin was headed home to see her boyfriend, David Reese. Landry's next movement, on the other hand, was less predictable.

As Santana hesitated, he asked himself whether he needed to inform Katz. After all, Lin was one of the rising stars in the U.S. Attorney's office and Katz would be devastated to learn that she was spying for the enemy, if in fact that was happening. Maybe, Santana thought, he should wait before jumping to conclusions.

The red taillights of her car vanished. Santana kept his post. Landry remained the focus of tonight's surveillance.

CHAPTER 13

An hour later, Santana sat in his car in front of the Principle Art Gallery on King Street, within eyesight of Landry's parked car. He had tailed Landry here from Crystal City. After Landry parked, he'd gone across the street to an Italian restaurant for dinner and then up a block to an Irish pub.

Santana considered following on foot, but quickly reconsidered. Most likely, Landry would spot him and that would raise a host of indelicate questions with the U.S. Attorney's office. For another, Santana doubted Landry was involved in anything nefarious and was simply enjoying a night out on the town.

A little before 1 a.m., Landry returned. He started his car and pulled out into the street without looking. There was no traffic. Santana waited over a minute and then followed at a safe distance.

Landry turned left by the Torpedo Factory and again onto Cameron Street. He drove a half dozen blocks through quiet residential streets to Washington Street, where he again turned left and proceeded across town in a southerly direction to the outskirts of the city.

Landry drove over the Beltway and proceeded to the stone bridge at the mouth of Big Hunting Creek, where Washington Street turns into an eight-mile stretch of the George Washington Parkway winding along the edge of the Potomac River to Mount Vernon.

Santana tailed him at a safe distance, roughly equivalent to two city blocks. City lights disappeared, replaced by the stillness of the back nine of the country club on one side and Belle Haven Park on the other, with deep woods all around. Dark brown trees created an even darker canopy over the highway, which was devoid of street lights below the stone bridge.

Santana was surprised by the route. He knew Landry well enough to know that he was a model of predictability, and this course was out of the ordinary. Santana had expected Landry to head to his apartment in Rosslyn, but instead he was travelling in the opposite direction at an odd hour of the night.

Without signaling, Landry executed a sharp turn less than a mile from the bridge to the road leading to the marina at Dyke Marsh.

However, he did not proceed to the marina. Instead, he turned left into the parking area for the Belle Haven Park.

Santana was caught unawares. He wanted to turn to pursue Landry, but there were no other cars on the road, and turning would draw Landry's attention. So Santana continued south on the G.W. Parkway, watching his mirrors as Landry's car drove the length of the parking lot.

At a break in the grass meridian strip a half mile ahead, Santana made a U-turn. Instead of doubling back, however, he pulled into a small rest area beside the road, waiting and wondering.

His first surmise was that Landry was having an illicit affair, a notion he quickly dismissed. He knew that Landry lived alone. There would be no scandal if he invited a man or a woman to his apartment. No one would care.

Then there were always drugs. Landry might be using illegal substances, Santana speculated. Yet it seemed unlikely that a law enforcement officer would arrange to conduct a drug transaction in a public park, knowing it was the type of location to be surveilled. The risk was too great.

Flummoxed, Santana pulled out of the parking space and proceeded at about 25 miles an hour. The headlights cut through the night. He removed his foot from the accelerator as he approached the park, and peered to the right.

The deserted parking lot was in the foreground. Next he saw empty picnic tables in the dark, their silhouettes visible against the backdrop of the river. Across the river, the neon Ferris wheel and lights of National Harbor emitted an array of colors.

Up ahead, where shore, river and sky melted into an indiscernible gray, Santana saw the majestic V-shaped crossbars of the Wilson Bridge spanning the Potomac River.

Brake lights flashed in the farthest corner of the park. Santana could see Landry exit his vehicle and walk down to the river. Barely moving at this point, Santana watched as Landry's shadowy figure crossed in front of the white façade of the Wilson Bridge. Suddenly, the lights illuminating the bridge went off. All was dark as the bridge faded into a grim shade of gray.

The absence of light was both a signal and a warning to Santana. He pressed the Fiat's accelerator and raced back toward Old Town. It was only a half mile to where the parkway turns into Washington Street and passes over the Capital Beltway.

**

Ten minutes earlier, large illuminated signs along I-95 announced to motorists that the drawbridge at the Wilson Bridge was being raised briefly for repairs.

CHAPTER 14

The roadblocks fell at 1:20 a.m.

Rows of white and red striped roadblocks dropped on both the Maryland and the Virginia side of the Potomac. The lights flashed just like the cautions at a railroad crossing. Then one half of the center span rose until it was nearly perpendicular to the highway, like a massive asphalt and steel palm raised for a high five.

Over 40 times a year, the largest drawbridge in the Interstate Highway System was tested to ensure its functionality. Years ago, the drawbridge was often raised to accommodate barges carrying materials to Alexandria and D.C., including *The Washington Post* print warehouses in Old Town. The *Post* facilities had been torn down and were being replaced by multimillion dollar residences, hotels, and shops. And the new Wilson Bridge, opened in 2006, greatly increased vessel clearance. Nowadays, the bridge was raised primarily for maintenance and only occasionally to accommodate vessels.

Traffic stopped at either side of the bridge. Given the curve of the bridge, the roadblocks, and the flashing signs, it was difficult to see what was happening beside the drawbridge. A half moon glowed overhead; from one angle, it appeared to be hanging on the tip of the raised portion of the drawbridge.

The lights that normally brighten the V shapes of the bridge's span were extinguished. It appeared as though the bridge had vanished, the result of a clever magician's trick. Water, land, and sky were indistinguishable from one another; everything was enveloped in blackness. Swiftly moving, low-hanging clouds veiled the stars and created an impenetrable screen.

Then large searchlights ignited the night on the bridge. A crane moved into position in front of the opening created by the raised drawbridge. A man dressed in a black leather jacket barked instructions to a crew standing around the crane.

A barge loaded with crates emerged from behind the canvas that draped the bridge with the large letters reading PASHA and floated to the half-opened drawbridge. The boom tilted like a steel giraffe as the jib lowered a cable to the barge. When the cable reached the barge, one of the crates was attached to its large steel hook. The machine's arm flexed its mechanical muscle and strained as it pulled the crate up. Minutes later, the rotex gear shifted and the crate was lowered onto a flatbed truck with a mighty thud.

Then the process repeated itself as the second of four trucks moved into position. The operation lasted about twenty minutes. When it was completed, the flatbed trucks drove with their cargo over the bridge's empty traffic lanes toward Anacostia. The drawbridge was lowered and the barriers raised to allow regular traffic to resume crossing the Wilson Bridge.

CHAPTER 15

The Beltway snaked under Washington Street south of the cemetery at the base of the Wilson Bridge. There were no ramps from the street to the bridge, although a walkway paralleling the lanes on the east side of Washington Street allowed access across the bridge.

Santana planned to go down the walkway. The electricity on the Wilson Bridge had been deliberately cut off and he needed to know the reason behind it. He slowed his car as he approached the walkway.

Three men stood at the entrance. They wore dark jerseys, black pants, leather jackets, and boots. Santana knew they would deny him access, so he quickly drove two blocks and turned right, ripping down blocks of quiet residential townhouses and shops and making several turns that brought him to Jones Point Drive.

He pulled into Jones Point Park, directly beneath the bridge, which towered overhead. From his car, he watched as the crane lifted its final cargo. Ten minutes later, the bridge lights came back on.

Santana exited his vehicle and walked to the edge of a pier extending from the parking area. The water smelled brackish in the still air. His eyes settled on the huge tarp hung from the top of the bridge to the water's edge advertising the name PASHA.

A moment later, he got back in the car and darted out of Jones Point. Eventually, he made his way to the entrance ramp to I-495, which dumped him onto the Virginia side of the Wilson Bridge.

The bridge had reopened. Moderate traffic was moving in the local lanes along the Outer Loop. In the express lanes, 18-wheelers stormed through the night, rushing to make up for lost time.

Santana knew it was hardly coincidence that Landry was at Belle Haven Park when the blackout occurred. The lights had been cut to hide clandestine activity on and beneath the bridge, including the use of the crane to lift crates from the barge on the water to the bridge.

Slowing the Fiat to a crawl, Santana pulled onto a narrow shoulder. A large SUV was stopped up ahead. Santana doused the car's lights. The brake lights of the SUV blinked and it moved forward, then into the flow of traffic, heading to Maryland.

Santana rolled the car to where the SUV had been stopped. He waited until the SUV disappeared and then turned on his emergency flashers to avoid being hit. He stepped out of the car. His feet landed on the metal teeth seamlessly fit together at the lip of the drawbridge.

"No ideas but in things," he said out loud, reciting a line by William Carlos Williams, the poet from Paterson, New Jersey, whose work he had admired in college. Those words were Santana's mantra in investigations. He brought no preconceived notions to a scene. True to Williams' principles of detection, the scene spoke for itself.

Santana looked around for clues. He pulled a small flashlight from his pocket and scanned the roadbed and curb, which were littered with shards of glass, cans, cigarette butts, papers, and slivers of wood. Something glittered among the detritus. "A Black Russian," he murmured, identifying the black paper and gold foil filter of a cigarette butt. He retrieved a pair of plastic gloves and a baggie from the trunk from the car, put on the gloves, and picked up the butt, placing it in the baggie.

He noticed a crane tucked against the jersey wall at the edge of the bridge. Orange cones were placed around it. He walked to the crane and felt the metal panel housing the engine. It was warm to his touch. He also noticed the fresh tire marks on the asphalt. Then he returned to the Fiat, where he carefully placed the baggie on the passenger seat before driving off.

He glanced at the time on the dashboard: 2:20. He headed home, knowing he would have to resume surveillance in the morning.

**

At 7:15 a.m., Santana, groggy from a long night's work, drove by Landry's townhome in Rosslyn. The driveway was empty. Santana stopped across the street for coffee, hoping Landry's car was parked in the garage.

CHAPTER 16

The Capitol was a beehive of activity on Thursday morning. Following the month-long August recess, members of the Senate and House resumed work with renewed vigor. Members walked across Constitution and Independence Avenues in the mid-morning sunshine. Others rode underground trolley cars to the Capitol from buildings named after titans and sentimental favorites: Russell, Dirksen, Hart, Cannon, Longworth, and Rayburn. Friends renewed acquaintances after the summer hiatus, while adversaries avoided encounters with partisan enemies. For members, staff, and the media, it was back to business as usual.

"Good to see you, Mac," the receptionist said cheerfully as the office's former chief legislative aide entered Senator Lowenstein's fourth-floor Russell Senate Office Building suite. They embraced. "Go right in," she said. "The senator's expecting you. Mr. Landry's already here."

McCarthy walked across the narrow reception area, its walls covered with photos of the senator shaking hands and smiling with presidents, potentates, dictators, dignitaries, and celebrities. The wall clock indicated 10:10. He knocked and then entered the senator's private office. No one sat at the large wooden desk in front of a large window framed with ornate blue and gold draperies. To the right, on either side of the thick carpet emblazoned with the seal of the United States of America, were Senator Lowenstein and Phil Landry. The senator was seated in the center of a leather sofa. Landry sat opposite, across a coffee table, in one of two chairs in blue leather with gold nailheads.

Landry was tired. He had slept less than four hours, rising at 6:30 and slipping out the door a few minutes after 7. He had an uneasy sense of being followed last night and wanted to avoid any possibility of being under surveillance this morning.

The senator rose. "I trust no one will grow suspicious of your absence," he said to McCarthy, who shook hands, nodded curtly to Landry and then parked himself in the empty chair beside Landry.

"I don't think Mac does enough work in the U.S. Attorney's office for anyone to notice he's missing," Landry said. It was a jab, but missed its mark. He was well aware of McCarthy's reputation as a prodigious worker on Capitol Hill and in the U.S. Attorney's office.

"From what I hear, the opposite is true," said Lowenstein, proudly. "In fact, I understand Mac is handling the BOM case." He paused, then added, "That's actually why I invited you here this morning. I'm a little concerned at the pace of the negotiations. You need to speed things up."

McCarthy's eyes shifted toward Landry. He suspected BOM would be the topic of discussion and that Landry would want information about the status of the case. "Katz has invested a lot in this case," McCarthy said. "And a lot of families expect to see BOM punished for its crimes. The case has to be wound tightly before we can step into final settlement negotiations."

"You have a conference next week," Landry interrupted.

"That's right," McCarthy said. "It's with Jane Hutton of Stephens, Babcock & Brazier."

"What's on the agenda?"

"It would be inappropriate to go into details about the case, at least without consulting with Mr. Katz. I'll just say we're feeling out one another, sort of like the opening stage of the competition."

"A competition, is it?" Landry asked in an insulting tone. "Aren't you speaking a little too cavalierly, referring to a major prosecution affecting a lot of our military like it's a sporting event?"

"Stop it, Phil," the senator instructed. Then, addressing McCarthy, he asked, "What about it? Where do things stand? Is the case likely to settle? Are any more people going to be charged in connection with the case?"

Rather than answering the question, McCarthy asked a question of his own. He made no effort to be deferential to his old boss. "Why are you both so interested? If there's something going on, I'd like to be informed about it."

"Need to know," Landry replied gruffly. "You don't have a need to know."

McCarthy turned to Landry. "If the senator is asking me for privileged information about the case, I have a right to know the reason behind it. Otherwise, you can ask someone else to do your dirty work.

Mo Katz selected me as a deputy U.S. Attorney, and I owe him a duty of trust."

"Oh, please," Landry scoffed. "Don't exaggerate your importance. Mo Katz had nothing to do with your going over to the U.S. Attorney's office."

Landry pointed to Lowenstein. "Here's the man who pulls the strings." He straightened himself in the chair and cleared his throat. Looking at McCarthy, he said, "You were put in your position to report to the chairman of the Senate Intelligence Committee, and don't ever forget it. Furthermore, don't be fooled by Katz. He's a two-bit defense attorney who's in over his head in that office."

Lowenstein interjected, "Everyone holds a position commensurate with his talents. I have never pushed for anyone to hold a federal position who was not qualified to do the job. It's as simple as that."

"If you say so," Landry said, rising. He knew he could not stay quiet if he remained in the room and that his continued outbursts would imperil any chance of McCarthy doing his bidding. "I've got an appointment. I'll leave the two of you alone."

After Landry left, Lowenstein said, "He's a hothead, Mac. He distrusts Mo and is afraid that a prolonged BOM case is going to impede his prize investigation. I have my doubts about those concerns, but it would be a shame if we didn't listen to him and he turned out to be right."

"What prize investigation?"

Lowenstein cocked an eyebrow. "Landry's running a sting operation to thwart a terrorist attack. It includes someone who's tangentially connected to the BOM case. That person wants to see BOM resolved for fear he could be implicated in the matter. Landry's just trying to put a confidential source at ease."

Lowenstein pursed his lips. "Landry's working against the clock. His operation is scheduled to culminate with arrests on the 17th of this month. He gets more anxious with each approaching day."

"So what do you want me to do?" McCarthy asked.

"Push it to resolution and settle the case." He shook his mane of white hair and ran a hand through it. "Use your imagination. You're an enterprising young man."

McCarthy hesitated. Then he said, "That line of Landry's about your putting me in Mr. Katz's office to do your bidding. I never thought of it that way. I've always assumed you asked Mo to hire me because I was the most qualified person for the job."

Lowenstein rose from the sofa. "Didn't you hear what I said a moment ago? I've never pushed for a person to hold a position who wasn't qualified for it. Never. That goes for everyone in this office and everyone I've helped secure a job elsewhere in the federal government, including you. That, my son, is the God's honest truth."

McCarthy nodded and pretended the matter was settled. "I'll see what I can do." Then he added, "It would be good if you told me more about this investigation. That's not too much to ask, particularly as it's being presented to me as a reason to fast-track a settlement of the BOM case."

Lowenstein nodded. "That's fair," he said. "But what I'm about to tell you is a closely guarded secret. Not even Mo knows about it. Landry needs free rein to succeed. Promise me you'll honor that." McCarthy nodded affirmatively. Lowenstein smiled as he sat down in the chair previously occupied by Landry.

CHAPTER 17

"About a year ago," Lowenstein began, "Landry hatched an undercover operation with a person of interest in the BOM case. Together, they enticed an errant group of foreigners to transport and store a large cache of illegal arms in Anacostia for a contrived attack on Bolling Air Force Base."

McCarthy's eyes widened. Joint Base Anacostia-Bolling – the official name for the old Air Force base – was strategically located below East Potomac Park in Southwest D.C. at the confluence of the Potomac and Anacostia Rivers, about a mile from the U.S. Capitol.

"Bolling no longer offers any actual protection," Lowenstein said as an aside. "During the Cold War, an air base adjacent to the capital meant something. Now it's a shell of its former self, good for employing a few thousand military and civilian personnel, but really nothing more than that, in my opinion. It's a relic of a bygone era, like Fort Washington."

"Got it," McCarthy said. He knew that Fort Washington, located five miles downriver, was constructed to guard the nation's capital from a British invasion up the Potomac River following the War of 1812 and the redcoats' burning of the White House. He did not consider the comparison an apt one, but said nothing.

"The illegal arms arrive on barges brought up the Potomac River," Lowenstein continued. "They're stored in a safe place and transported to the warehouse in Anacostia. Later this month, after the final shipment arrives, Landry is going to expose the sting operation and arrest the entire crew of would-be terrorists."

McCarthy thought about places where terrorists either attempted or succeeded in creating havoc at military installations: the planned attack at Fort Dix, the carnage at two military installations in Chattanooga in 2015, the rampage at Naval Sea Systems Command HQ at the Washington Navy Yard in Southeast D.C., and the 2009 shootings at Fort Hood that resulted in 13 fatalities and more than 30 injuries.

"It's been a carefully managed operation, tightly controlled from start to finish," Lowenstein said. "A phony overseas shipment company was devised to make it appear as though the arms were coming from

Germany or Russia. False bills of lading were created at Hampton Roads."

"Impressive," McCarthy said. He had a gnawing feeling this fact pattern might lend itself to a defense of entrapment. In the worst case scenario, the feds found a bunch of stooges, concocted an imaginary plot that appealed to the stooges' warped sense of reality, and then staged a takedown that appeared to save the nation from another 9/11. In the best case scenario, the feds identified some sociopath hell-bent on sending mail bombs to political leaders or shooting up a synagogue and captured him before he could carry out his insane plan.

"Landry has latched onto some real badass dudes," Lowenstein said. "They're killers and thugs intent on doing the nation real harm. It'll be good once they're convicted and put away for life."

McCarthy appreciated the confirmation of the plot's legitimacy. "How did Landry sell the plan to them?" he asked.

"He reminded them of Malaysia Airlines Flight 17, which was shot down over Eastern Ukraine five years ago in July 2014, probably by a BUK-M1 missile," Lowenstein explained. "Landry sold the co-conspirators a phony story about how they could cause the same havoc in Washington."

Next, McCarthy asked a series of operational questions. "What happens to the shipments when they come upriver? How are the arms moved? Where are they stored?"

Lowenstein paused. "I'm not going to provide you with any more details, Mac. I've told you too much already. Phil would be upset if he knew I'd shared any information at all with you."

McCarthy changed topics. "What about the connection to BOM?"

"The person of interest came across Landry's radar during the early stages of the BOM investigation. That's all I know."

McCarthy knew the details of the BOM case better than anyone. If Landry had found a person of interest and pulled that person out of the inquiry to pursue this sting operation, McCarthy was confident he could figure out that person's identity.

"I think maybe we should slow down the case, identify this person of interest, and figure out the extent to which he's implicated in BOM," McCarthy said.

Lowenstein furrowed his brow. "Sometimes you don't listen, Mac. Why don't you just follow instructions? Wrap up the case and be done with it. Don't forget who brought you to the dance."

McCarthy lowered his head. "I haven't forgotten," he said. "I'll do what you ask, even if it feels like a betrayal of Mr. Katz and his office, and even if I think we should be taking the opposite approach." He tried to sound convincing. "I don't like it but I'll do it. You've been my benefactor and I'll do your bidding."

Lowenstein was too experienced to miss the insincerity in McCarthy's voice. "Look at me," he said. McCarthy raised his head but avoided looking directly at his old boss. Lowenstein studied his former aide. "Okay," he said, finally. "Do what you feel you have to do. Do what you think is right."

Then Lowenstein shifted in his seat and smiled. "What's your prognosis for the Nats?" He knew McCarthy was a diehard Nationals baseball fan who followed the team as passionately as Lowenstein studied political trends and poll results.

McCarthy took the bait and the two talked baseball for the next ten minutes. Lowenstein simply wanted to end the conversation on a high note. After McCarthy departed, the senator's smile disappeared as he stood at the large office window overlooking Union Station. His view was obstructed by scaffolding set up to restore the façade of the Russell Senate Office Building.

The senator was not particularly impressed with himself. He had capitulated to Landry's demands and tried, at least for a minute, to manipulate the actions of one of his protégés. It was all wrong. Landry was obsessed with the case, and the possibility of something going terribly awry seemed more likely every day.

Lowenstein opened his office door and addressed the receptionist. "Get U.S. Attorney Katz on the phone. Ask him to drop over to my office next Monday, first thing in the morning. And don't put it in the calendar."

CHAPTER 18

When Landry left Capitol Hill, he took the 3rd Street Tunnel to I-395 and drove to the 14th Street Bridge past the Jefferson Memorial and across the Potomac River. Traffic was moderate at noontime. He stayed in the right lane and took the Clark Street exit, swooping down the exit ramp by the Pentagon and onto a stretch of State Route 110 that led him under the 14th Street Bridge.

Landry turned right at the end of a T-shaped intersection and drove by a public storage facility. He pulled to the curb, put the car in park, and checked his phone for text messages. He found the one he wanted, which simply read: HERE. He turned off the car, got out, and walked across soccer fields to Long Bridge Park, bordered on three sides by the Potomac River, Roaches Run, and the Pentagon lagoon.

He spotted a burly man with close-cropped hair smoking a cigarette and staring at his iPhone. He approached the man slowly and cautiously. "Hello, Alec. How did it go last night?"

Alec Gordievsky looked up and pulled the cigarette from between his lips. He flicked the ash off and stuck the cigarette back in the corner of his mouth. "The entire shipment in the warehouse, like other times," he replied in broken English. The cigarette butt bobbed up and down as he spoke. "We ready for final shipment next week."

"Good," Landry replied.

Gordievsky pulled the cigarette from his mouth and exhaled. "Then I'm finish."

Landry smiled. He detected fatigue on the part of the young Russian. "You're finished when I say you're finished," he said. "We have a deal. If you try to pull out now, I will hunt you down and send you back home. Do you understand?"

Gordievsky pressed his thin lips together and tossed the cigarette onto the ground.

"I'm glad we understand one another," Landry said. "I have invested significant resources into this operation. You and the others have a job to finish for me."

Gordievsky coughed. He removed a cigarette pack from his back pocket.

An airplane shot up into the sky from Reagan National Airport, a quarter mile away. Both men paused and stared at it while it climbed at a steep angle. Gordievsky raised the hand not holding the cigarette pack, formed a gun, and mimicked shooting the plane.

Landry disregarded the gesture. "Anything else?" he asked.

"Nyet." Gordievsky pulled a cigarette from the pack and lit it with a cheap lighter. He took a puff and sent a plume of smoke into the air.

Landry looked at the ground, hiding his inner thoughts. Although Gordievsky and the other Russians involved in his operation were not Russian military intelligence, Landry viewed them as the same ilk as those arrested for hacking at the Organization for the Prohibition of Chemical Weapons in The Hague; leaking World Anti-Doping Agency drug test data; spying on the investigation of MH17, the passenger plane hit by a Russian missile in eastern Ukraine; and poisoning Sergei Skripal and his daughter in Salisbury, outside London. They were evil and could not be trusted. It was only a matter of time before Landry would have to beat Gordievsky into submission to command his loyalty.

"Alright, then," Landry said. "Talk to you later."

**

Just as Landry disguised his true feelings, so did Gordievsky. The Russian had tested one of the weapons in the warehouse and discovered it was a dud. As a result, he questioned Landry's identity and intentions. Gordievsky was confused and conflicted about almost everything, with one exception: he knew he wanted out.

CHAPTER 19

Landry remained in the park after Gordievsky departed. He watched birds flying along the river bank. Something was wrong. He could sense it from Gordievsky's attitude, which bordered on insubordination. He wished the sting operation could be launched tomorrow.

Landry returned to his car and weaved his way through Crystal City to the nondescript square cement building that served as his headquarters.

Ten minutes later, he was standing in the conference room. The model of the Wilson Bridge dominated the table behind him. Pencil-size gates were lowered on either side of the drawbridge near the center of the bridge. One half of the drawbridge was open like a trap door. A yellow model crane was parked on the unopened half, its jib hanging over the opening. Four model flatbed trucks were lined up beside the crane and pointed toward the Maryland shore. Photos of the bridge were posted on the walls around the room.

Seated at the table and standing against the wall were over a dozen members of the antiterrorism task force handpicked by Landry.

Landry grabbed a pointer. "Early this morning," he began, "a shipment of illegal surface-to-air missiles was successfully delivered to a warehouse in Anacostia. As with previous deliveries, the arms arrived in Norfolk via Charleston, where they were hauled up the Potomac and unloaded onto a barge hidden behind a tarp on the Wilson Bridge."

Everyone watched as he extended the stick to a section of the model covered by a brown piece of paper on which was written the word PASHA. Using the pointer, Landry pulled out a piece of cardboard from behind the brown paper and slid it across the table. A red wooden block sat on top of the cardboard. He moved the cardboard under the open portion of the drawbridge.

"The barge was unmoored and positioned beneath the drawbridge," he continued. "Half of the drawbridge was raised and the crates filled with arms were lifted by crane and loaded onto flatbed trucks. The trucks moved across the bridge and delivered the arms to the warehouse in Anacostia."

To illustrate his point, he reached across the table, picked up the red wooden block resting on the cardboard, and placed it on one of the model trucks. As he pushed the truck across the bridge with the pointer, he said, "While traffic heading onto the bridge will be backed up in front of the gates, there won't be any traffic on the other side of the drawbridge, so the trucks will move unimpeded."

The model truck with the red block traveled across the bridge and onto the shiny surface of the conference table. A look of satisfaction spread across Landry's face. He put down the pointer and looked at the members of his team.

"A week from tomorrow, on Friday, the 13th, the final shipment is going to arrive. It will be placed on the barge, which will remain hidden beneath the bridge behind the tarp. And on Tuesday, the 17th of September, we will load the arms onto the trucks in the middle of the afternoon.

"While the drawbridge is open and as the crates are loaded onto the trucks, a massive takedown operation will commence. Under your direction, counterintelligence forces will strike from the air, land, and sea. Simultaneously, we will take custody of the arms stored at the warehouse."

Landry felt immense pride welling up as he concluded, "Operation Open Sky will be underway."

No one in the room locked eyes. If they did, it would give away what was running through many of their minds. True, they thought, the feds had a name for every major operation, like Crossfire Hurricane for the investigation into Russian meddling and Abscam for the '70s operation in which congressmen accepted bribes from Arab sheikhs belonging to a dummy company called Abdul Enterprises. And then there was Operation Varsity Blues for the college cheating scam. But Operation Open Sky for a Landry-run operation?

To the seasoned operators in the room, it was a pretentious name for a contrived operation. It was a well-known secret that Landry was using it as a stepping stone to head the Department of Homeland Security. No one liked the fact he was turning a staid security operation into a Hollywood production or that he was using the chairman of the Senate Intelligence Committee as a foil for personal gain.

Landry was oblivious to those concerns. He acted as though the only sound he heard was their applause. "Any questions?" he asked, heaving with pride.

One of the few women in the room spoke up. "If the final delivery arrives next Friday, why not swoop down in the early morning Saturday and take them out? Isn't it going to draw suspicion to wait until the following Tuesday and undertake the operation in broad daylight?"

Landry's response was brisk and dismissive. "The terrorists are not the least bit suspicious," he scoffed. "Once they're on the bridge and the gates are down and the drawbridge is up, it's like a steel trap. They've got nowhere to go."

Landry waited a second. "Any other questions?" The room was silent. "That being the case, the meeting is adjourned. I request that you continue drilling at the Memorial Bridge and elsewhere. Know your part of the operation. Operation Open Sky is fast approaching."

As they filed out, the woman who had asked the question found herself next to one of the seasoned veterans. "Don't feel bad," he told her in a low voice. "The man's an ICBM." She looked at him quizzically. "Insecure, conceited, bombastic megalomaniac," he chuckled. "I've been with Landry for five years. Nothing he does surprises me anymore."

"It's not funny," she said. "As I understand it, the only reason he's delaying until the 17th is because he wants the takedown to coincide with a patriotic celebration."

The veteran nodded. "Landry's got tall ships sailing up the Potomac. The media will all be assembled. It's going to be a show."

"It's too much," the woman warned. "He better not drag us all down if this operation gets fouled up. And there's something about it that's starting to worry me."

CHAPTER 20

Late Thursday night, David Reese sat alone in a large room on the second floor of the Alexandria Police headquarters off Duke Street. The large windows along the far wall stared out at a nearly empty parking lot. Twelve desks covered the floor, separated by beige sound barriers. Papers, phones and computer terminals sat atop each desk. For safekeeping, case files were locked in cabinets and desk drawers. The night shift was out on the street, and the day crew was at home for the evening.

Dressed in a green T-shirt and blue sweatpants, Reese opened *Modern Criminal Procedure* by Kamisar, LaFave, Israel, King, Kerr and Primus, a staple of law school students for over a generation. He might as well do some reading, he figured. Tonight was the first night of his internship with the Alexandria Police Department, a part-time gig arranged by his girlfriend's boss, Elmo Katz.

Sherry Stone, his supervisor, parked him here two hours ago. She left in a foul mood after taking a personal call. Reese respected other people's privacy but couldn't help hearing her rip into the caller for cancelling a date the previous night.

If nothing else, he had already learned to avoid getting on Stone's bad side. He figured that would serve him well for the entire semester. She didn't look like the type of woman to mess around with, he concluded.

The desk phone rang. Reese looked around. After the fourth ring, he picked up the receiver.

"Hello," said the voice on the other end in a husky, tentative voice. "I'd like to report some suspicious activity, or at least I think it's suspicious."

"This is the Alexandria Police Department," Reese said.

"No kidding, Sherlock," replied the voice on the other end. "That's why I called you instead of Luna's restaurant. Or do you not investigate suspicious activity? Maybe I got the wrong place."

"Okay," replied Reese, grabbing a pen and pad lying in front of him. "Your name, please."

"Can I just give you my first name?" the caller asked.

Police protocol probably required a complete name, Reese presumed. But he also felt that the caller would hang up if he was insistent. "That's fine," he said.

"Frank."

"Okay, Frank. What have you got for me?"

"I haul construction materials by barge up the Potomac from Hampton Roads, Norfolk, and Chesapeake to the District," Frank began. "There have been a few times recently that something weird happened."

"What's that, Frank?" asked Reese.

"Usually after we're just north of the Occoquan and approaching the Wilson Bridge, a motorboat pulls alongside the barge. A big one. People get on board. The crew is pulled off. We're taken to shore and the barge continues up the river. I've been barging off and on for years, and it's never happened before." Frank sounded worried. "We also get some extra pay for our help, which I consider as some sort of hush money."

Reese looked around for Stone or one of the night shift's detectives. No one had returned. "What do you think is going on?" he asked.

"I think someone's moving drugs," Frank replied. "Maybe heroin or cocaine, like those operations they just busted in Baltimore and Philly. I don't know. I'm guessing." He hesitated. "What do you think is going on? You're the cops, aren't you?"

"Could be any number of things." Reese scratched his head. "What can you tell me about the shipments?" he asked, scribbling notes.

"Normal, you know. Crates from Hamburg, Rotterdam, Liverpool. I'm not sure where else. They arrive in Savannah or Charleston, or maybe Columbia Bay, and then come to Hampton Roads, where they're loaded onto a barge and moved upriver. Heavy stuff. Too big for trucks and too bulky for trains."

"Do you know who's in charge of the operation?"

"No idea," Frank replied. "We're just the crew. We just haul it up the river."

"Who are these deliveries addressed to?"

"Some of it goes to Pasha, I think," Frank said.

"Who's that?"

"It's a small construction company. They've got a huge tarp with their name on it hanging from the bridge to the water, doing some sort of construction."

"How do you spell that?" Reese turned his paper sideways as he ran out of room. Frank spelled out the name and Reese wrote it down in capital letters.

"I certainly agree this is odd," Reese said. He hesitated, then asked, "Would you be willing to meet with me and another investigator and show us where the motorboats meet the barge? We could drive the George Washington Parkway up from Mount Vernon to Alexandria. I'm familiar with the area."

"Okay," Frank replied. He sounded enthusiastic at first, then slightly panicked. "I'm not sure about tonight."

Reese laughed. "I wasn't thinking about tonight, either. How about tomorrow?"

"Sure. Okay. That's fine."

"I'm going to need to call you back. What's your number?" Frank recited his phone number and Reese repeated it. "Okay, Frank. I'll call you sometime tomorrow afternoon. We'll arrange to meet along the parkway and get this sorted out."

Reese jotted down some more notes and waited for Stone to return.

**

An hour later, Reese closed his book, packed his bag, and headed out. Despite calling Stone twice, Reese had been unsuccessful in locating her. He knew he should have left long ago, and hoped his girlfriend, Mai Lin, wasn't annoyed by his repetitive texts announcing his imminent departure.

As he left the building and walked toward his bike, Reese spotted Stone standing against the side of the building. She was puffing on an e-cigarette. He walked in her direction. She tucked the cigarette into her bag as he approached.

"Do you have a minute?" he asked.

She removed ear plugs, pulled her phone out of her pocket, and turned it off. "What did you say?" He repeated his request. She had a contented look in her eyes. "Yeah, let's go inside," she said. They went through the main entrance. Before they reached the elevator, Stone opened a side door and took the concrete stairs two at a time. Reese followed to the second floor.

Stone headed to a small corner office with a wall of windows facing the large room where Reese had been sitting all night. The room was now occupied by two officers seated at desks facing one another. The officers didn't look up as Stone and Reese walked by.

Once they were seated in her office, Stone said, "I listened to your messages. They were cryptic, but you're obviously concerned about something. What's up?"

"I got a weird call from a guy who works barges that come up the Potomac," he said, explaining the situation described by the caller.

"You waited until midnight to tell me that?" she asked.

"Yes," Reese said. "I think he identified something, but I don't think it's drug-related. Narcotics flow up the interstate. The routes are established. There's no reason for someone to ship large quantities of drugs up the Potomac River to D.C. I'm convinced it's something else, maybe weapons, which are heavy and bulky."

Reese expected Stone to be angry and tell him not to answer the phone or, if he did, to refer calls to investigators. He also expected her to remind him that the river was not in the city's jurisdiction and belonged either to Maryland or District authorities. He was not prepared when she asked, "Did he tell you when the barge came up the river?"

"No," he said.

"You sound surprised. Why's that?"

"Honestly, I expected you to tell me to drop the matter."

"Quite the contrary," Stone said. "It might be coincidental, but a friend was just telling me about a weird happenstance at the Wilson Bridge early this morning. The drawbridge was opened for a short period of time. The lights on the bridge went out while the span was open.

"So when you mention the bridge and a company doing construction on it, and some sort of contraband being shipped up the river, I wonder if it's connected with the drawbridge. Probably not, but it's an odd coincidence. You've got the name of the guy who called?" Reese nodded affirmatively. "Good. Tomorrow or next week let's give him a call and gather a little more information on this whole thing. Now go home to that girlfriend of yours."

**

It was 1:30 on Friday morning when Reese returned to his apartment. He didn't turn on any lights. He went to the bathroom, removed his clothes, tiptoed down the hall, and slid under the sheets.

"Where have you been?" asked Lin, turning her lithe body and gazing at him. "I was worried. You didn't even text me that you were going to be late."

"I was investigating an incident," he whispered to her. "Someone might be shipping drugs or guns or something up the Potomac around the Wilson Bridge. I'm working with Ms. Stone. She's pretty cool."

Lin touched his cheek. Then his hair. "I love you," she said. "I'm glad you're not hurt or anything."

"I love you, too," he answered.

They cuddled and fell asleep in one another's arms.

Life could not be better. Once Reese graduated from law school, he would become a prosecutor. Then Lin would begin law school. When she finished, one of them would get a job that paid big bucks. They would buy a house. Somewhere along the way, they would marry and start a family. It was all mapped out. It seemed nothing could mar their dream.

CHAPTER 21

Katz could hardly suppress his surprise when he received a call mid-morning Friday from Matthews. "I thought you were in Columbia Bay," he said.

"We had an abrupt change of plans."

Katz wondered if they had returned early because of Hutton's scheduled meeting with his office next week. "Weren't you supposed to be down there for a week or something?"

"Yes, but we got robbed," Matthews explained. "I tried to call you the night it happened. I guess you didn't receive it."

Katz remembered the call he disregarded in the middle of the night. "What happened, exactly?" he asked.

"I'll tell you about it at lunch."

"Lunch? I don't know about that, Sean. I've got a busy day. It's Friday."

On Friday, trial work was set aside as judges handled a full slate of sentencings and civil and criminal motions. The prosecutor's office was operating in overdrive on this day. Nonetheless, Matthews persisted. "I don't think you understand, Mo," he said. "I almost got killed the other night."

Part of Katz wanted to protest, but it didn't take much cajoling for him to relent. Truth be told, Katz liked Matthews. Even if their formal partnership ended quickly, a personal bond endured. After all, Matthews had offered Katz a launching pad for his private practice. Katz was indebted to Matthews and could not be dismissive toward him.

Ninety minutes later, they were seated at the counter of a deli at Rosslyn Circle eating pastrami on rye and drinking iced tea. Katz was dressed in a blue pinstripe suit. Matthews wore a T-shirt, sweat pants, and sneakers.

"It was the most harrowing experience of my life," Matthews said. "I didn't expect to survive. It scares me even now talking about it."

Without any encouragement from Katz, Matthews reconstructed the scene.

"We're having dinner," he began. "Everything's going fine. Well, not fine, exactly, but good enough. Jane was being a bitch, but that's par for the course. Anyway, I paid in cash and we were leaving the restaurant when this guy comes up behind us. He said he was going to rob us. Jane started shaking. My heart was pounding.

"The voice said, 'Sean, reach into your back pocket. Remove the roll of bills. Hold it behind you. Don't turn around.' He said he had a gun. I did exactly as I was told." Matthews adopted a Darth Vader voice when he repeated the robber's words.

"I was afraid we'd be robbed and shot or forced into a car, taken down a dead-end street, and then shot. Or maybe directed to go to an ATM and withdraw additional money, and then be forced into the car and shot. You know?"

Matthews looked at Katz for a sympathetic response. Then he resumed eating his pastrami on rye.

Katz gave him a couple of minutes and asked, "Then what happened?"

"The man snatched the money from my hand," Matthews said. "In a really menacing voice, he asked if that was all my money. He started ordering me: 'Pull out your wallet. Give it here. Don't turn around.' I slid my wallet out of my inside jacket pocket and held it behind my back. The guy grabbed it from my hand.

"He kept telling us not to look around. A second later, he was gone. After a minute, Jane and I turned around. I was literally gulping air, like I'm being held underwater for too long. Then we both screamed at the top of our lungs. 'Help! Robbery! Help!' We screamed like a couple of banshees."

Matthews' face was flushed. Katz noticed perspiration forming on his forehead. Matthews drank half of his iced tea and took another big bite out of his sandwich. Then he resumed the story.

"People materialized from all directions, rushing down sidewalks and out of buildings. Twenty people, maybe more, rushed toward us.

"I pointed at the side street. I told the crowd, 'I think he took off in that direction.' An instant later, someone hollered, 'There he is!' About a block away, a crowd gathered. We ran toward it. In the middle of the crowd, two men were on the ground, tangled up with one another.

"One of the men was hollering, 'Get off me.' He had a reedy voice. The crowd kept him on the ground while the other man got up. The crowd decided which one of them was the robber, I guess."

Matthews fell silent. He remembered seeing his wad of money and wallet on the ground, and reaching for them. Someone said he should just leave it as evidence and let the police dust everything for fingerprints. He complied. The last thing he wanted was to be accused of tampering with evidence.

At the time, he wondered what to say if the police asked about the source of the money. Lying to Hutton was one thing, but lying to the local authorities was something else. After all, he was an officer of the court.

"Someone in the crowd summoned the police and within minutes an officer arrived," Matthews continued, shaking his head. "Steve McBride, the man identified as the robber, was handcuffed. I couldn't see his facial features—it was too dark. He was protesting the whole time, claiming he was innocent. The other man, the one they let go, identified himself as Kevin Chalk. I remember thinking at the time he looked a lot like a piece of chalk: thin and pale white.

"Backup arrived and McBride was taken into custody. A police officer put on a pair of gloves and picked up the money and wallet. I was asked to come down to the station and give a statement."

Matthews finished his sandwich. A waiter refilled the iced tea and Matthews thirstily emptied the glass. "No one thought to question Jane," he said, sourly. "She went back to our place to go to sleep instead of going with me to the station. When I got home, I learned from her that someone had broken into our room while we were out. Fortunately, nothing was stolen. I was too tired to report it."

Matthews ran his tongue over the front of his teeth. He reached his hand into his mouth and tried to pry something loose with a thumbnail. "It destroyed our vacation and probably our relationship," he said. He shook his head from side to side. "I don't know, Mo. I went down there with such high hopes. Everything was going so well. And now this."

Katz said nothing. He had lots of questions but decided now was not the time to ask them. He suspected some crucial details were omitted, like the origin of the cash. Mentally, he filled in the empty spaces in the narrative as a seasoned prosecutor would do.

The waitress removed their empty plates and placed the check on the counter. Katz picked it up. Matthews offered to split the tab, but Katz refused.

"Did they lift any prints?" Katz asked.

Matthews shook his head. "You know it's almost impossible to get prints off bills. Plus they were all wadded up, which made it even harder. I thought they might get lucky with the wallet, but no dice. They kept photos of everything and returned the cash and wallet to me."

"What about the firearm?"

"None."

"Were you able to ID McBride as the robber?"

"No. I never saw his face during the incident, and his face was all in shadows at the time of the arrest. They never showed me a photo spread or lineup either."

Katz mulled that over for a minute, then asked, "Are you telling me all they've got is someone in a crowd calling one of the two men out as the robber?"

Matthews understood the problem with the case. "Someone in a crowd who didn't see the robbery," he added for emphasis.

"Without prints or a confession, or an eyewitness coming forward, I don't know how anyone can make this case," Katz said. "I doubt a grand jury will even return an indictment." He looked at Matthews, who nodded in agreement.

CHAPTER 22

They left the diner and walked to the parking lot. Traffic swirled around Rosslyn Circle, some cars exiting to cross the Key Bridge into Georgetown and others taking the ramp to the Roosevelt Bridge or the Pentagon and Crystal City. Still other cars proceeded toward Ballston.

Matthews asked awkwardly, "Did Abby tell you about the case after we ran into one another the other night?"

"What case?" Katz asked evasively.

"About the praecipe."

"Yeah, as a matter of fact, she did." He assumed Snowe would not mind his sharing a confidence in this instance.

"What did she say?"

"Not much, other than that you disposed of a case without consulting her."

Matthews laughed. "You were always better at dishing out the truth than lying, Mo." He leaned into Katz. "I know what she told you. That I'm a scumbag who perpetrated a fraud on the court and earned her eternal enmity for it. Am I right?"

Katz smiled. "Yeah, something like that."

"Do you believe her?"

"I suppose I do."

"I'm sorry to hear that," Matthews said. "Let me tell you what really happened. One day in District Court, a police officer handed me a praecipe for a suspended imposition of sentence and told me to give it to the judge. I did as I was asked. Snowe saw it and thought I was pulling a fast one on her. Actually, the officer was running a scam on behalf of some petty misdemeanants. He was getting favorable dispositions for them in exchange for a few bucks on the side. It wasn't even one of my clients."

"Okay," Katz said, wondering about the identity of the officer. They stopped beside Katz's car. Katz opened the door and got in. Before he shut the door he looked up at Matthews. "Who was the officer?"

Matthews hesitated. "I don't remember," he said evasively. "It was a long time ago."

Katz started his car. "If you remember, let me know," he said. "I'm curious to know who it was."

"I'm not lying," Matthews said. "What I told you is the truth."

As Katz started to drive away, Matthews hollered at him. Katz rolled down the window. "Hey, if there's a trial and I have to testify, will you go down to Columbia Bay with me? This whole thing is freaking me out."

Inwardly, Katz rolled his eyes but said, "I'll give it some thought."

**

Katz took the G.W. Parkway to get back to Alexandria. The lagoon yacht basin was on his right. As he drove over the stone bridge that fed water from the Potomac into the lagoon, the 14th Street Bridge appeared on the left.

Katz observed two large black rafts offshore filled with men and women wearing orange life jackets. The occupants of one raft wore red helmets, and the occupants of the other wore blue helmets. Both rafts bobbed beneath the bridge.

It appeared to be a safety or security exercise, but Katz could not recall ever seeing emergency management teams practicing at this location. The other day, he had seen a similar exercise conducted directly north of the airport runway adjoining Gravelly Point, a half mile south.

As he drove under the 14th Street Bridge, his thoughts were diverted by a car switching lanes to maneuver to the ramp to Reagan National Airport. He switched mental gears and started thinking again about the BOM case.

He would focus on the case all weekend. There would be time to go jogging; do a few chores around the house; fill the fridge with groceries; drink coffee and read the weekend *Wall Street Journal* and the Sunday *Post* and *New York Times*. Mostly, however, he would work on BOM.

He had the entire weekend. He glanced at the time on the dashboard: 2:15 p.m. Abby was already up north with her mom, he thought to himself. He hurried back to the office.

**

As Matthews drove back to his office, he received a text from Prolokov. He pulled to the side of the road. It was an invitation to Saturday brunch. Matthews rarely received such offers and, when he did, he always refused. It was bad form to get too close to a client, to create a bond and actually care about an outcome, particularly since most cases went south in the end.

Yet, in this case, he decided to forgo his own best advice. After all, Prolokov was a corporate client. That made it okay, he concluded, texting back his acceptance.

CHAPTER 23

Early Friday evening, Jane Hutton called Jon Bennett, an attorney recently retired from the public sector who was defending McBride in the Columbia Bay robbery. "Hey," she said. "How are you?" She lit a cigarette as she paced on the sidewalk outside her office building. She did not listen to his response.

"Listen," she said. "I need a favor. I do not want to get sucked into that robbery case, Jon. I didn't pay the bill. I didn't chase anyone. I didn't see or say anything. I just don't have the time for it. Okay?"

She casually knew Bennett from his years in white-collar crime at the Department of Treasury. She listened patiently to his response. She recalled how he could be a total pain in the ass.

She sucked on the cigarette, coating the filter with her lipstick. "No," she said, "I don't even want to be on any list of possible witnesses. I need to be cut out of the picture entirely. There is absolutely no reason on earth to consider me."

Hutton felt trapped. If she wanted to convey a message to defense counsel, the smarter course of action was going through the prosecution. But then the prosecution might ask her to testify. Since she had not heard from the prosecutor, she decided to let sleeping dogs lie and handle it on her own.

"I haven't made a final decision on the witnesses I intend to call," Bennett confided. "I've got to figure it out quickly, though, now that my client's only facing a misdemeanor."

"A what?" she asked, shocked at what he had just said. She took another drag on the cigarette and listened as Bennett explained how he persuaded the prosecution to reduce the charge from a felony robbery to a larceny misdemeanor.

"That's fascinating," she said. "I guess that's how you handle justice in a small town. You could never get away with it up here. I mean, it's just incredible." She took another drag excitedly. "At this point, you can't lose. Even if your client is convicted, there's no comparison between a felony and a misdemeanor. It doesn't get any better than that."

But it did. The prosecutor had agreed to a bench trial, Bennett bragged.

"Bravo!" she bellowed. "Bravo!"

It suddenly occurred to Hutton that she had jumped the gun. If Bennett had gotten the charges reduced and fast-tracked the case as a bench trial, then he would probably want as few witnesses as possible. After all, it came down to the credibility of the two main characters in the case, Sean Matthews and the reputed robber.

"Has the prosecution contacted you?" he asked.

"No," she answered. "Nobody's contacted me to testify in the case-in-chief or as a possible rebuttal witness."

He kept probing.

"Oh, come on, Jon," she implored. "I am not the star witness. Give me a fucking break." Then she softened her tone. "Listen, just forget I was ever there and handle the case without me. Do it as a professional courtesy, alright?"

Out of nowhere, he asked her about Matthews.

"We've split," she said. "Something happened at Columbia Bay. We cancelled our trip and came home early. I'm through with him." She laughed at his next statement and replied, "In your dreams."

The conversation shifted to the BOM case. Hutton had no problem sharing some of the details with Bennett. She calculated that treating him to a few tidbits might endear her to him and increase the chances he would agree to drop her as a witness in the case.

"We've got a conference with the U.S. Attorney's office in a few days," she confided. "Between you and me, I'm going to push for endgame. My client's given me a figure to settle the case."

She blew smoke as she listened to his banter. "No, I'm not going to share the amount with you, but it's generous, in my view, a clear indication the client wants to bring the case to a conclusion without any more damaging headlines." She squared her shoulders. "Yes, of course I think I can settle below the ceiling. After all, who do you think they're dealing with?"

Bennett asked who was managing the negotiations from the other side.

"Some pipsqueak who used to work up on the Hill. He got his position as a political favor. Abe Lowenstein's his daddy, from what I hear. I'm going to crush his balls."

After a little more banter, she said, "Okay. Great. Thanks. I owe you one." She hung up the phone and threw the burning cigarette into the street.

CHAPTER 24

It was the Saturday morning after the Labor Day holiday and the city pulsated with activity. From Rock Creek to the G.W. Parkway, joggers and cyclists took to the streets in bright shirts and black stretch pants. Couples pushed strollers along streets and through parks. Logan Circle and Capitol Hill were crammed with people out for brunch, walking dogs, going to the Eastern Market, and enjoying the beautiful day. The H Street corridor vibrated with activity as office responsibilities gave way to more mundane priorities like trips to dry cleaners, gasoline stations, barber shops, and food markets.

In Georgetown, streets and sidewalks rekindled their acquaintances with the previous night's revelry. Singles and couples shuffled to coffee shops and corner stores. By 11 a.m., all the clothing store doors were open for business.

Inside a bistro on Wisconsin Avenue above M Street, Prolokov sipped a Bloody Mary and wished for a cigarette. He was dressed in an open-collar white shirt, blue blazer, slacks, and loafers without socks. He waited for Matthews.

Brunch was intended to be an ambush. Prolokov had originally planned the event to extract information from Matthews about his girlfriend, Jane Hutton. But he had heard the couple had recently separated. Hence, Matthews was no longer any use to him.

When Matthews arrived, they retreated to an upstairs table. Matthews was wearing the same T-shirt and sweatpants he'd worn the previous day. He ordered eggs and steak frites; Prolokov asked for a gravlax omelette and a Belgian waffle. Matthews drank mimosas. Prolokov selected Smirnoff on the rocks with a slice of lemon.

"I am no longer be in need of your services," Prolokov said after their meals were served. "I overestimated the cost of having a registered agent. According to a business associate, it is not as complicated as I assumed. In fact, it's rather simple."

Matthews dropped his fork. He was relying upon Prolokov's retainer as though it was an inheritance from a rich uncle. He had not expected such a gift, but now he was loath to part with it. He grabbed his napkin and wiped his mouth. "Suit yourself, Boris, but good legal advice is hard to find," he said.

"I don't disagree," Prolokov said. "But good advice is honest advice. You should have advised me there was no need for such a high retainer for a registered agent. If you had done so, I might not be inclined to cut our ties now."

"How about we cut it in half?" Matthews asked.

Prolokov smiled. Lowering his head, he fixed his eyes on Matthews and said, "I'll think about it and let you know on Monday."

**

Two hours later, Prolokov wobbled to his Mercedes parked on Wisconsin Avenue. He got into the car, pulled out and turned left onto Prospect Street, drove a block past restaurants and townhomes, and made another left on Potomac Street, which swooped down to the light at M, where he turned right. He intended to drive to Foxhall Road, but inadvertently got caught in the middle lane, which forced him to turn left across the Key Bridge and across the river to Virginia.

"Son of a bitch," he muttered under his breath. He pulled out his phone, touched an app, and sought directions back to the District. A soothing voice instructed him to stay in the far lane and turn left at Gateway Park and then swoop around the circle to the ramp for the Roosevelt Bridge.

He followed the instructions until he saw a sign for the Key Bridge next to the sign for the Roosevelt Bridge. He recalculated the route and made another left turn, executing a complete circle back into Georgetown. He switched lanes without signaling or making any effort to merge safely into the traffic coming down Lynn Street.

As he made the turn, the Mercedes struck a car in the adjacent lane. The next instant, police lights and a siren punctured the carefree early afternoon atmosphere. Prolokov pulled to the curb; the car he struck pulled in behind him. He waited as the officer, who parked in front of the two other cars, approached.

"License and registration," the officer asked.

"I'm sorry, officer," he said. "It's just a small fender-bender. I'm clearly at fault. I'll pay the other driver for the repairs to his car, and then some. I'd like to avoid having it reported to my insurance carrier."

"License and registration, please."

He puffed on his cigarette before snuffing it out in the ashtray, which was already filled with cigarette butts. He fished a wallet out from his back pocket and pulled out his license. He handed it to the officer. "I do not have a registration," he said slowly, his speech slurred.

"Mind if I look in there?" the officer asked, pointing to the glove compartment.

Prolokov turned and stared at the glove compartment. "This is a rented vehicle. I do not have a registration. But, no, I don't care if you look in the glove compartment. I know a little about the law."

"I'm sorry?"

"I do not own the car," Prolokov said. "So, if you find something in the glove compartment, like a handgun or a bloody knife, you can't connect it to me." He chuckled.

The officer stood back from the door. "Have you been drinking, sir?"

Prolokov stared at her, knowing that vodka does not give off an odor. "No," he said.

"Please step out of the car, sir."

A second squad car pulled up and parked. Two officers approached.

"I don't think this needs to be turned into a capital offense," Prolokov said. "I'm willing to pay the other driver for all of his bother and expenses. Can we just settle this between ourselves?'

"Please step out of the car, sir."

The other officers were now standing on the passenger side of the car. Prolokov calculated what to do. How many drinks had he consumed? If he passed the field sobriety tests, could he still be taken into custody? Would he be offered a breathalyzer now? If so, he would fail it. If he was placed under arrest, would he to be able to call an attorney? When? Would they ask for a blood sample? If they did, should he refuse?

"Sir, please exit the vehicle."

A third cruiser was now pulling to the curb.

Prolokov opened the door and got out of the Mercedes.

"How much have you been drinking, sir?"

"I have not been drinking," Prolokov said. "I have done nothing wrong. I am perfectly sober. I want an attorney."

**

Prolokov walked out of the Arlington police station four hours later. The field sobriety tests were ridiculous. Walking the ten spaces, pivoting, and walking back. Doing a one-legged stand with his hands out on either side of him, like an airplane. And touching his nose. He thought he had passed all of them. And what about rejecting the breathalyzer at the scene? Why was that grounds to place him under arrest for DWI *and* refusal?

He turned to Matthews, who walked beside him. "Thank you for coming so quickly and getting me out on bond," he said.

"No problem," Matthews replied, grateful for the unexpected call and positive turn of fortune. "I'm your attorney. That's what I do." Maybe now, he thought, he would be able to keep at least half of the original retainer.

"This was an absolute outrage," Prolokov said. "A humiliation."

"I agree," Matthews said. "It's going to be okay. You never submitted to a breathalyzer or a blood test. I don't think they can get you for a DWI. You were switching lanes in heavy traffic and barely scraped that other car. You'll be convicted of a refusal and you'll lose your privileges to drive in Virginia for a year. That should not be a problem."

Prolokov snorted.

"The car was impounded," Matthews continued. "We'll have to get it out."

Prolokov muttered under his breath. He did not care whether the car was impounded. It was a rental car. Let them keep it forever. He turned to Matthews. "What happens next?"

"We'll go to court on Tuesday for the arraignment. We'll enter not guilty pleas to all offenses and set a trial date. Before the court date, I'll have this case worked out for you. For openers, I'll find the driver of the other car and we'll work out an attractive settlement with him. If it's attractive enough, he won't show for court. And, if he's not there, it gets a little hard for the prosecution to win the case."

They headed to Matthews' car. Each man was consumed in his own thoughts. Although they walked side by side, their thoughts were light-years away from one another.

CHAPTER 25

Early Monday morning, Katz arrived at Senator Lowenstein's office. Traffic was heavy heading into the District, this being the first full work week after the Labor Day holiday.

Katz was indebted to Lowenstein. Following the murder of former U.S. Attorney Helen O. Douglas two years ago, the senator recommended Katz as the federal prosecutor for the Eastern District. Katz expected the senator to extract a quid pro quo in exchange for the nomination, but Lowenstein never sought one. There were, of course, some small requests along the way, such as hiring McCarthy, but Katz never considered such favors to be of much significance in the scope of things.

Katz had heard the same rumors as everyone else that Lowenstein recommended him because he was a political lightweight. It was true that he harbored no ambition to use the office as a political springboard, but he never doubted he handled the job like a pro, racking up a series of high-profile convictions. The BOM case would only add luster to his list of impressive achievements.

Katz went through security and used the staircase to reach the fourth floor. Lowenstein alighted from the elevator just as Katz bounded through the stairwell door. They greeted one another and walked together to the senator's office.

Once in Lowenstein's office they sat down facing one another in the blue leather chairs. It took only a few minutes before the senator brought up Landry's name. "We go way back together, over thirty years," he said. "It pains me that two of my favorite people can't get along with one another. Promise you'll work at it."

Katz and Landry had butted heads when Landry was a cop and Katz a defense attorney. Even before that, actually, back to when Katz was a prosecutor, or so Katz recollected. Landry's arrogant and egotistical manner rubbed Katz the wrong way and made the attorney suspicious of the cop's every move.

Two years ago, in solving the Daingerfield Island caper, Landry took a bullet in the lung and held Katz responsible for it, even though

Katz was not at fault. That incident sealed their relationship, or so Katz concluded. From that point forward, there was only bad blood.

"Senator, there's no way Phil Landry and I are going to repair our rift," Katz said. "We're polar opposites. He thinks my tactics sabotage the criminal justice system and I eye everything he does with suspicion. Nothing is going to change that."

Katz eyed Lowenstein, who shifted impatiently in his chair. Katz realized he was not here to be lobbied to get along with the head of the antiterrorism task force. Something else was going on. "You didn't invite me over here to discuss my relationship with Landry, did you?" Katz asked. "What's up?"

"In the coming days, you're going to hear reports of MANPADS being shipped to the District of Columbia," Lowenstein began somberly.

Katz's eyes narrowed to dark slits. Man-portable air defense systems were illegal for a reason. Armed with one of those lethal shoulder-launched surface-to-air missiles, a homegrown violent extremist could turn a city block into something resembling a swath of Lebanon, Libya or Syria.

"You give one of those to the kind of people who left their mark at the Boston Marathon, San Bernardino, or Oklahoma City, and you've got a real problem on your hands," Katz said.

Lowenstein casually shook his head. Despite being the bearer of distressing news, the senator did not appear to Katz to be particularly alarmed. Katz could only draw one inference from the senator's nonchalant manner.

Katz stood and walked to the window. Staring out at the obstructed view of Union Station, he tried to connect the threads of their conversation to reach some fast conclusions.

"This isn't clandestine ops, it's a sting operation," Katz said, thinking out loud. "And it involves Landry. Everyone knows he doesn't actually uncover plots, he concocts them. He doesn't actually save anyone from terrorist threats so much as fabricate threats and grab headlines.

"He doesn't need to coordinate a plan with other agencies in the metropolitan area if all he's doing is laying the trap. He can act like a lone ranger. If the defendants cry entrapment, it's not his problem; and if the case goes south, he'll use the attorneys as scapegoats, claiming they botched the prosecution."

Lowenstein stood. Katz walked over to him. They faced one another eye to eye.

"You're giving him free rein for some reason," Katz said. "Maybe you owe him one, or maybe it's intended to advance his career, or maybe it's just good for business. You know, keeps the public worried about a terrorist menace that can only be defeated with taxpayer dollars going to special interests that fund your Senate campaigns."

"Hold it right there," the senator warned sternly, holding up a hand.

Katz stared hard at the senator. "Forgive me if I disregard the stop sign, but I'm going to drive right through it. You called me in here for a reason, Abe, and I'm going to give it to you straight. If my suspicion is correct, you're actually afraid Landry's gone rogue, or close to it, and that he may be creating a situation more dangerous than the one he's pretending to stop."

Lowenstein raised and lowered his eyebrows, took a deep breath, and pursed his lips, but he did not acknowledge a thing. It was obvious he was not prepared to lay down another card.

"What can I do?" asked Katz.

"Do your job. Keep your eyes open. If something comes up, use whatever resources you have at your disposal to make sure everything turns out the right way."

Katz nodded. He had the old man's back. "Will do," he said.

"Oh, and you're coming Wednesday morning?" Lowenstein asked. "I've got a seat for you in the V.I.P. section. And be on time. It's not the sort of event for which you can be late, as is customarily your wont."

"Yup," Katz said as he left the office.

**

Once outside, Katz recalled how frustrating it was to deal with Lowenstein. Getting to the truth was like opening a set of Matryoshka dolls. Katz had to open one clue after another to understand Lowenstein's real intention.

He called Santana when he got to his car. "Are you still attending those antiterrorism group meetings with Landry?" he asked. Katz started the engine and backed the car out of the space.

"No, but why do you ask?"

"I just met with Abe Lowenstein. He started out asking me to make nice with Phil Landry. He ended up acknowledging he's worried that Landry's gone rogue.

"Landry's in charge of some sort of sting operation involving illegal arms brought into the District, according to the senator. He didn't share any more details, probably for fear I'd blow the lid off the thing."

As he spoke on the phone, Katz maneuvered into traffic and headed back toward Alexandria.

"Like I said the other day, there's a connection, Curtis," he said. "Lowenstein was providing just enough information to whet my appetite. He wants me to keep an eye on Landry."

Santana listened intently. "I'm already on it," he said. "After our last conversation, I followed Landry, like you asked. He ended up along the G.W. Parkway below the Wilson Bridge, playing sentry as the drawbridge was raised in the middle of the night. It was a very freaky scene. At one point all the lights on the bridge went off, just about the time Landry arrived."

"Do you think there's a connection between the bridge closing and Landry's sting operation?" Katz asked.

"No doubt, but I'll be damned if I know what it is."

The conversation went silent. Mental dead ends greeted both of them. More pieces had to fall into place before it was possible to make sense of anything.

"By the way, what are you doing tonight?" Katz asked. "Abby's gone home to see her mom and I don't want to spend the night alone drinking Port City lager on my porch."

"Wish I was free, but I've got a date."

Katz was surprised. "With who?" he asked.

"It's private. I'd like to keep it that way, if you don't mind."

"Somebody I know?" Katz persisted.

"Maybe," the investigator answered.

Next Katz called a few old friends, including an Arlington cop and the Alexandria sheriff, none of whom was up for a boys' night out. Eventually the list narrowed to one last name. "Yeah, sure, Mo," Matthews answered when Katz called. "Wherever you want to go, whenever is good for you."

CHAPTER 26

Late Monday, Reese returned to the Alexandria police station, wearing jeans and a Washington Capitals sweatshirt depicting the Stanley Cup, a tribute to the home team's 2018 championship season. He put his backpack on the floor, opened his criminal procedure book, and picked up the phone. All weekend, he had dialed the same number unsuccessfully. This time, someone answered.

"Hello, Frank?" Reese asked excitedly. "Frank, is that you?"

"Who is this?" a male voice asked after a prolonged silence. Frank knew it was Reese. He had avoided the guy's persistent phone calls and messages all weekend. On reflection, he regretted calling the police. If something bad was going on, it was dangerous for him to blab.

"This is David Reese," the eager voice answered. "You called about goods being shipped by barge up the Potomac River. We are supposed to meet, remember?"

"I can't meet after all," the man replied.

Reese was silent for a moment. Then he said, "I traced your phone number on the Internet. Your name is Frank Morelli. I also checked your police records. You've been in and out of jail for petty misdemeanors, and you have one serious felony charge that went to trial and resulted in a dismissal."

"You're not supposed to be doing that shit," Morelli said angrily. "That's an invasion of privacy. You've got no business looking into my private affairs."

"It's all publicly accessible information," Reese said matter-of-factly. "I didn't use any police databases or anything like that. It's nothing for you to be embarrassed about. As far as I'm concerned, it says a lot about you, Mr. Morelli, calling the police because you're suspicious about what's going on along the river."

Morelli softened a bit. At least the kid knew he was on the up-and-up. Maybe he could atone after all, he thought.

"Plus," Reese continued, "I read about your trial and know you were represented by Mo Katz. I worked on a case for Mr. Katz a couple of years ago."

"That so?" Morelli said, beginning to relax. "Mo's good. *Fatta la legge, trovato l'inganno.* That's his motto. It's Italian for 'The law has more holes than a chunk of Swiss cheese'," Morelli chuckled.

"That's close, Frank, but not exactly right. It means 'For every law, there is a way around it.' The law's not porous, although there are ways around it, just like there are ways around mountains if you're smart enough to know how to hike in that environment. The law itself is actually impermeable."

"Whatever," Morelli said. "I thought you were a cop, but you sound more like a lawyer."

"Not yet, but I will be in a couple of years. And I'm going to work for Mo Katz, whether he remains U.S. Attorney or goes back into private practice. I'm just interning with the police."

"Stay with the best," Morelli instructed, wishing he had listened to similar advice when he was a younger man.

"So," Reese said, lowering his voice, "have there been any repeats?"

"No, I learned my lesson. Mr. Katz forced me to get into a rehab program and paid for my therapy when I fell back off the wagon."

Reese was silent for a moment. Then he said, half-embarrassed, "I mean the barges. Are there any more shipments planned?"

"Oh, yeah, right," Morelli laughed. "In fact, yes there are. My foreman wants me back in Norfolk by late tomorrow. We have a new delivery for later this week."

"Really?" Reese watched as Stone entered the office, going into the small office where they had spoken last weekend. She was dressed casually in jeans, black stiletto heels and a tight black leather jacket over a magenta blouse.

"Listen, my supervisor just came in," Reese said. "Let me go talk to her and call you back. Maybe there's something we can do to trace the shipment."

Reese hung up the phone and hurried down to Stone's office. "I just spoke to the guy who was on the barge," he said after exchanging hellos with her. "He's going back down to Hampton Roads, says he's got a new shipment to deliver in D.C. in a couple of days."

Without asking for any more explanation, Stone told Reese to get back on the phone with the informant. She hopped on the call and introduced herself.

"Stevie Stoner," Morelli said a minute later. "How the fuck are you?"

Stone glanced at Reese, who pretended not to hear or care. "I'm fine, Frank. You taking care of yourself?" She hit the mute button and said, "I was the arresting officer in a case with him. Morelli was a crazy motherfucker when he was your age."

Then she unmuted the phone. "David's told me about the barges. I agree it's some strange shit, probably drugs. Are you willing to take a risk and help us?"

"Why not?" Morelli said, changing his tune.

"Good," Stone said. "We're going to need a warrant, Frank. Once that's done, we'll get some tracers for you. They're small devices, magnetic and easy to hide. When the crates leave the barge, we'll be able to track their route and figure out where they're delivered."

"This will be a bit of a crapshoot. You understand that, right? I mean, I can't guarantee we're going to find anything."

"Life is a roll of the dice," Stone replied. "You just got to hope you're lucky. You're feeling lucky, aren't you Frank?" Then she asked Morelli to meet her at the U.S. Attorney's office first thing in the morning.

"You mean in Mo Katz's new office?" Morelli asked.

"That's right," Stone replied. "His office has jurisdiction for things like this. Plus, it'll be like old times, us getting back together, except we'll be on the same side this go-around."

When the call ended, Reese said to Stone, "Luck is when preparation meets opportunity."

"I'm sorry?" she asked.

"The Roman philosopher Seneca said that," he explained. "You said luck is something that you hope for, but there's really no such thing as luck. Either you're ready when the moment presents itself, or you're not. It's as simple as that."

She smiled, shaking her head, not realizing how prophetic his words would prove to be within a week's time.

CHAPTER 27

First thing Tuesday morning, Stone, Morelli, and Reese huddled in McCarthy's office. Stone explained a possible scheme to ship drugs into the city via the Potomac River. Morelli supported her theory.

McCarthy sat in stupefied silence. This wasn't about drugs, he knew. He was learning the details of the operation that Lowenstein had withheld from him.

McCarthy believed he could legitimately issue a warrant based on probable cause that drugs were being shipped up the Potomac even though he personally knew something else was taking place. After all, he concluded, no one would have cause to challenge the legitimacy of the warrant. And, with the information gathered through the warrant, he would acquire more details about Landry's operation.

McCarthy said nothing about this to the others. He would level with them when the time was right. That moment had not yet come.

"What specific facts can you give me about drug smuggling?" he asked Morelli. "For example, is there suspicious activity at the dock when you take on the materials to ship up the river? What conversations have you overheard? Were there discussions among members of the crew? Did you discover drugs when you prowled around the crates, maybe open one or two containers? Things like that."

"Nothing more than what she just told you," Morelli said, nodding toward Stone.

"Well, then, repeat what she said," McCarthy said.

When Morelli finished, McCarthy filled out an affidavit to accompany a request for a warrant. The affidavit read as follows:

"Based upon information from a confidential informant, your Affiant has been apprised of the existence of a major drug smuggling operation being run along the Potomac River, utilizing barges carrying industrial materials to ferry narcotics, specifically heroin, into the Northern Virginia area.

"On two separate occasions, the CI has participated as a crew member on a barge on which several pallets containing drugs

were loaded. When the barges approached Northern Virginia, speedboats came alongside and the crew was ordered to offload portions of the cargo. The barges are believed to have continued upstream, diverting to the Anacostia River, where the remainder of the drugs were unloaded at an undisclosed location on the District waterfront."

"Good enough?" he asked as Stone and Morelli read it.

"Yeah," Morelli replied. "It's better than good enough."

Stone smiled slyly as she signed the form. "Let's find a judge," she said.

Thirty minutes later, the four sat in McCarthy's office with a signed warrant and two tracking devices. "You're going to have to hide them under the lip of a couple of the crates, okay?" Stone asked.

"Yeah, that shouldn't be any problem," Morelli said tentatively.

"Here, let me show you how these work," she said. "There's nothing to it. These devices are magnetic. They're already activated. You just slip them in. Piece of cake."

"Okay," Morelli agreed.

McCarthy picked up the phone. "Ms. Lin," he said. Reese stiffened in his seat. "Can you please come to my office and escort a person down to a conference room at the end of the hall?"

A second later, Lin stood in the doorway. "David," she said. "I didn't expect to see you here." Everyone looked from her to Reese and back at her. "David's my fiancé," she explained.

Morelli turned to McCarthy. "Sweet Jesus," he said. "We're just one big happy family."

CHAPTER 28

Across town, Matthews accompanied Prolokov to his arraignment on the DWI charge. Matthews had upgraded his T-shirt and sweatpants to a tweed sport coat, brown pants, a blue shirt, and red tie, although he hadn't quite lost his rumpled look. Prolokov was dressed casually in a crisp open-collar white shirt, black slacks and a light blue cashmere sweater. Of the two, he had a more polished style.

"You won't have to say a word," Matthews explained as they entered the atrium of the Arlington courthouse and rode the escalator to the second floor. "The judge will ask how you plead. I'll say, 'not guilty.' Then we'll set a trial date and walk out."

A moment later, they entered the District Court through large oak double doors. Court was already in session. Matthews recognized the judge, grabbed Prolokov by the arm, and hurriedly turned him around. He escorted Prolokov to a cushioned bench beside a wall of windows facing the street.

"I'm going to recommend a slight change of plans," he advised his client.

"What are you talking about?" Prolokov asked uneasily.

"There's a substitute judge on the bench," Matthews explained. "He's a close friend of mine and very favorably disposed to the defense bar. If you enter a plea today, I'll request the case be continued to his sentencing docket.

"When you return for sentencing, I'll present evidence about how you're rehabilitated. The judge will probably knock down the DWI to reckless driving and impose a fine, maybe order a short suspension of your driving privileges. And he'll dismiss the refusal charge."

Prolokov shook his head. "No," he said. "I don't want any fuss today. My rental car is in the impoundment lot. I'm not getting it back. Just do what you said you would do in the first place, enter a plea of not guilty. Then we go, okay?"

"You're not listening to me," Matthews insisted. "I'm confident you'll come out of this without a DWI conviction. You just have to trust me."

Lowering his voice, Prolokov whispered an emphatic "No."

"Suit yourself," Matthews replied, irked that the client was not following his instructions.

They returned to the courtroom. When the case was called, a plea of not guilty was entered and an October date was selected for trial. Prolokov's unsecured bond was continued. They walked out of the courthouse, down the escalator, and back onto the street.

Matthews was visibly annoyed. "You should have listened to me," he said. "If all you want to do is plead guilty, maybe you don't even need an attorney."

Prolokov smiled. The arms shipment was scheduled to arrive on Friday. They would lift it from the barge onto flatbed trucks on the 17th and store it in the warehouse. A few days later, missiles would rain down on the military base. If everything went according to plan, he would be comfortably out of the country by that time. He had no intention of returning to court in October.

CHAPTER 29

At 11 a.m. on Tuesday, a call was placed to the U.S. Attorney's office from Stephens, Babcock & Brazier. Senior partner Jane Hutton, counsel for the Bank of Magellan, was confirming Thursday's meeting. Word spread throughout the office that Hutton herself was on the phone. The way people reacted, it might as well have been a call from the president or the pope, or Beyoncé.

Katz had McCarthy take it. He trusted his senior litigator implicitly. As he watched McCarthy pick up the phone, a look of contentment swept over Katz's face. It had been a long time coming. *The harder they come, the harder they fall.*

BOM was once the standard-bearer in business entrepreneurship that handled the securitization of some of the most prestigious international commercial real estate and industrial capitalization deals in the world. Over time, hairline cracks in the bank's impeccable image appeared. It failed financial stress tests, an unimaginable result for a too-big-to-fail entity. Next there were rumors from the European Union that BOM had manipulated the Euro vis-à-vis the dollar, the pound sterling, the ruble, and the peso.

As the dominos fell, bad went to worse. Allegations that BOM was an accomplice to state-sponsored terrorism were investigated. Working with the families of young soldiers killed by improvised explosive devices in Iraq and Afghanistan, Katz and McCarthy discovered that the terrorists who planted the IEDs were trained in Libya and that the funds for the arms and the training flowed from a labyrinth of financial institutions originating with BOM.

"Excuse me, coming through," Lin said, getting by Katz. He had been daydreaming, recalling the months of painstaking work involved in the chase. Now a new chapter in the hunt was unfolding. Either BOM would capitulate or it would be war. Lin held a file in her hand.

"Mac left his file in the conference room," she said, turning to Katz as she hurried down the hall. "Where would that man be without me?"

**

McCarthy was finishing the call with Hutton as Lin entered.

"I hope you didn't need this for the call," she said, handing the file to him a moment later.

"No," he laughed. "Hutton called to psyche me out, that's all. It's a typical maneuver. I've been expecting it."

Lin was about to ask what Hutton had said when McCarthy's personal cell phone rang. He put up his hand, indicating that she did not have to leave. McCarthy motioned to the door, and she closed it. Then he turned on the phone's speaker. Lin did not catch the words that were spoken, but she recognized the voice. It was Phil Landry.

"I'm sorry," McCarthy said. "What was that? I didn't hear you." Of course, he had heard precisely what Landry said, but wanted it repeated for Lin's benefit.

"She's not coming over on Thursday to be confrontational," Landry repeated. "She's going to offer to settle the case. So be prepared."

"How do you know that?"

"I've got sources," Landry said scornfully. "Good sources, I might add. So start thinking about terms and conditions. Bring it in for a landing, kid."

"Don't push too hard, Phil. If you do, I'm likely to move in the opposite direction."

"I doubt you'll do that, not after what the senator said," Landry replied.

"You have no idea what we talked about," McCarthy said. "I'm my own man. I don't take direction from Abe Lowenstein and I certainly don't take it from Phil Landry."

Landry scoffed. Then he said, "By the way, did you send that Chinese or Vietnamese girl, whatever she is, over to Crystal City the other night to pick up some research materials?"

McCarthy glanced at Lin. "Yeah, why? Did the two of you run into one another?"

"I'm surprised she didn't tell you anything about it," Landry said. "She's a nice girl. Don't get her mixed up in something that's too big for her, or you'll both regret it." Then he hung up.

"What was that about?" Lin asked, ignoring Landry's insulting comment. "Who does Landry think he is, talking to you like that? 'Bring it in for a landing, kid.' He sounds like a complete imbecile."

McCarthy looked at her carefully. He wanted to know what she was doing in the Crystal City building where the antiterrorism task force had its offices. To get her talking, he told her that Landry had tried to pressure him to settle the case, while leaving out pertinent details, like meeting in Senator Lowenstein's office and learning about the person of interest in the BOM case.

As he hoped, Lin reciprocated. "I haven't told anyone this, but I went to Crystal City to where Landry's antiterrorism operation is housed. I appreciate your covering for me."

McCarthy accepted her thanks with a dismissive nod. He wasn't interested in her thanks. He wanted her to share her information.

"It was strange," she said. "There was a model of the Wilson Bridge on a large table in the main conference room. Landry was sitting there, staring at the model of the bridge.

"I asked him about it. He said there are some tall ships coming to Alexandria and they're going to raise the bridge and he's overseeing all of the security operations. The thing is, I didn't believe a word of it. I think he's doing something else."

McCarthy asked, "What possessed you to do that in the first place?"

"Mr. Katz is suspicious of Landry's motives. I overheard him expressing his concerns to Curtis Santana. So I sort of took matters into my own hands."

"Running a little clandestine operation," McCarthy laughed. "That was gutsy. Have you shared your discovery with the boss?"

"Not yet," she replied.

"Maybe we should keep this between ourselves, at least until we have a better understanding of what's going on," McCarthy advised.

Lin stared at him. "Do you think there's a connection between the drugs being shipped up the Potomac River and Mr. Landry's surveillance operation on the Wilson Bridge?" she asked.

"Maybe," McCarthy replied slyly. "But right now we need to stay focused on the BOM case. Once that's resolved, we can come back to this."

"Okay," she agreed.

"And I'm sorry about the way Landry characterized you," McCarthy added.

"It's not your problem," she said. "You don't have anything to apologize for." Mac's comment sounded insincere to Lin, which made her wonder whether he was withholding information from her.

CHAPTER 30

"Mr. Katz, thank you so much for joining us for dinner," Lin said as she opened the door around 8 p.m. She took the bottle of Merlot he handed her, looked at it, and said, "This will go perfect with dinner."

Katz was still huffing slightly as he entered the apartment. Lin and Reese lived on the top floor of a three-story building in Arlington's Fairlington Village. The brick and slate-roofed townhomes and apartment buildings had been constructed by Italian masons in the early '40s as part of the war effort and converted into condominiums in the '70s.

Lin gave Katz a quick tour of their unit, which had two bedrooms and a loft. A sofa sat alone in the living room across from a big-screen television. Their bedroom consisted of a queen-size bed with no headboard and a single white wooden bureau that they shared. A desk and office chair occupied the other bedroom. The loft contained a half dozen large pillows, clustered together on the wooden floor. Despite the Spartan furnishings, the apartment was warm and inviting.

The three of them sat in the small dining room nook next to double doors that opened onto a small patio. On the floor was a large volume of the *Collected Works of William Shakespeare*. Lin said she was going to read all of the bard's plays, beginning with *Hamlet*.

At the end of dinner, the bottle of Merlot sat on the table, half-full. Reese and Katz had each had a glass, but Lin hadn't touched a drop. "I've got some important news," she said, looking at Katz.

"What's that?" Katz asked.

She held out her hand and showed off her engagement ring.

"Wow," Katz said. "This is fantastic."

"It was spurred by an unexpected development," she said, glancing down and rubbing her belly.

"Mai!" Katz exclaimed. "This is absolutely wonderful news." Reese, who had retreated into the kitchen, appeared holding a pot of coffee. Katz stood and heartily patted him on the back. Then he leaned over and hugged Lin. "I'm so happy for both of you. I had no idea. When is the baby coming?"

"I'm just finishing my first trimester," Lin glowed. "We're getting ready for March Madness," she laughed.

"Have you told others?"

"No, I'm going to wait another month or so, although I think people at the office will put two and two together pretty soon, even without me saying anything."

For an instant, it seemed as though Lin wanted to share something else, but then the moment passed.

Reese poured coffee for Katz and himself, then sat down next to Lin, wrapping his arms around her. "We're so blessed," he said. "Meeting you was one of the best things that ever happened to us, Mr. Katz. Mai loves her job. My internship in the Alexandria police department is going great, and so is law school. We're confident it's the right time to start a family."

"Of course it is," Lin said, leaning into Reese. "It's absolutely the best time."

CHAPTER 31

Wednesday morning, a bright sun hung in an azure sky. Flags stood at half-mast, flapping in a stiff breeze. For people of a certain age, the cloudless blue sky and crisp autumn air reminded them of the morning of September 11, 2001, a clear, beautiful day that would be disrupted by a seismic event that shifted the geopolitical, societal and cultural plates underpinning the world.

Katz sat in the V.I.P. section at Department of Homeland Security headquarters listening to Senator Lowenstein speak at the podium.

"I was in my office in the Russell Senate Office Building on that fateful morning," Lowenstein said. "I was planning a trip to New York City in advance of the mayoral primary. I was actually going over a speech I was scheduled to give in a couple of days, a speech that was never delivered."

His hands tightened on the sides of the podium. "There are few days that are seared in my mind, but 9/11 is one of them. Like the assassinations of Jack and Bobby Kennedy and Martin Luther King, Jr., the explosion of the space shuttle, and the day a madman tried to take Ronald Reagan's life, I remember where I was and what I was doing. And I know it left an indelible mark on my life."

The time was now 8:40 a.m. Everyone old enough to remember knew it was six minutes before the moment that American Airlines Flight 11 crashed into the World Trade Center's North Tower. Less than 20 minutes later, the South Tower would be hit. Then the Pentagon at 9:37 a.m. And finally the crash of United Airlines Flight 93 in Shanksville, Pennsylvania.

"The remarkable thing is that, horrendous as it was, that attack had some positive aspects for me and for our nation," Lowenstein said. "It renewed my commitment to devote myself to public service and, at least for a time, it brought our nation together."

As Katz listened, he reflected on his life the way people often do at funerals. He was a freshman at college in 2001, heading to class when the word swept across campus. His own decision for public service was forged that day as well, though the route to his current position had been circuitous and unpredictable.

"9/11 created this department," Lowenstein continued. "It placed responsibilities under the federal government that had previously been in the purview of the private sector. It drove home the realization that there are people out there intent upon doing us harm, and that it is our responsibility to find them and to stop them before they can carry out their evil designs."

At 8:46 a.m., Lowenstein stopped speaking. Heads were bowed. The same happened in lower Manhattan, at the Pentagon, in a field in Pennsylvania, and throughout the country.

An hour later, Katz was back at the office, working.

**

In the afternoon, Matthews received a call to return to Columbia Bay the next day for trial. He was floored by the news. The felony had been broken down to a misdemeanor. A judge would hear the case, not a jury. And the maximum penalty was 12 months in jail, not 20 years in the penitentiary. Part of him wanted to chuck the whole thing, but he agreed to catch an early morning flight.

He called Katz to vent. "No one was courteous enough to check if I was okay with reducing the charge," he said. "I mean, no one bothered to even discuss the case with me. And here we are, on the eve of a bench trial. It's ridiculous."

Katz tried to be polite and patient. He sympathized with Matthews. He also tried desperately to get off the phone. He had a lot on his mind.

Then Matthews leaned on him. "I need you," he implored Katz. "You have to go down there with me. Please. I gave you a job when you left the prosecutor's office and didn't have a place to hang a shingle."

Katz rebuffed the request. "Listen, Sean, I can't get away. We have a meeting scheduled with Jane Hutton. I'm trying to get this case across the finish line. I can't walk away from it tomorrow."

Matthews would not let go. "I realize how important BOM is to you. But you have Mac handling it. He's a good attorney. Let him do his job."

There was silence, the kind that almost forced Katz to inquire whether Matthews was still on the line. Then came the whimpering.

"I'm scared, Mo. I don't know what's going to happen. I did some foolish things that night, like going to Columbia Bay with too much cash in hand. If things go the wrong way, I'm going to be in trouble."

"I'm the U.S. Attorney, Sean. I can't hold your hand on something like this."

"You're my friend, Mo. Maybe my only friend. And our friendship predates your appointment. I've never asked you a favor in my entire life, until now. I need you, and you owe me."

CHAPTER 32

Thursday was overcast. In the small southern coastal town of Columbia Bay, local merchants were slowly returning to life without tourists, putting out signs advertising half-off sales and conducting inventories of items that remained on shop shelves. Hammocks, outdoor furniture, grills, and other merchandise were brought indoors, while bathing suits and summer clothes were put in boxes to be shipped to discount outlets.

The amount of traffic driving along the main street had dwindled to a fraction of the summer's volume. At the outskirts of town, an officer was replacing the "2" with a "3" on the posted speed limit sign, letting the locals know they could resume driving at 35 miles an hour. The revenue from speeding tickets was about to drop precipitously.

Matthews walked to the courthouse, located between a hardware store and a Methodist church. It was an antebellum structure, with high ceilings, fan-shaped windows, and ornate benches in the lobby. Two tiny courtrooms were situated opposite one another on the main floor, accessible from a lobby with a worn marble floor.

The building reminded him of courthouses in rural Virginia. The lobby was filled with all the usual characters: cops, defendants, witnesses, family members, courthouse employees, and attorneys. It was the same crowd that gathers every day in every courthouse across America.

Outside one of the courtrooms, Matthews met the arresting officer. A woman stood next to him. "I'd like you to meet Ellen Gahagan, the prosecuting attorney," he said.

She was tall and stocky, dressed in a light grey skirt and white blouse, and wore no makeup or jewelry. She was holding a burgundy briefcase. "We have a few minutes to prepare your testimony," she said.

The trio stepped into a small windowless anteroom. Gahagan closed the door. She placed the briefcase on a bare table pushed against the far wall.

"I know it looks like we haven't given your case much attention," she conceded. "I'll be honest. We didn't think we'd get an indictment from the grand jury. Defense counsel was willing to knock down the charge to a misdemeanor and proceed to a bench trial. I figure it's the best we can do.

"If he's convicted, it's a crime of moral turpitude, so it'll have some lasting effect. We've got a tough judge, which is both good and bad. She's going to expect strong evidence to render a finding of guilt, but if she convicts, she'll throw the defendant in jail for 90 days or more."

Matthews nodded his head in agreement. "You take what you can get," he said. The detective must have told her about his outburst yesterday, Matthews assumed. He was okay now; he just wanted the case to be over.

Gahagan opened the briefcase. Inside was a paper bag with a sandwich sticking out, a black Mont Blanc pen, a long yellow legal pad, and a thin file labeled *State v. McBride*. She removed the file and the three of them settled into worn wooden chairs around the table.

"I read your statement," she said. "It was filled with important tidbits, like the fact you and your girlfriend quarreled over dinner about whether you brought formal attire." She cast an accusatory glance at the investigator, who pretended not to notice. "The level of police work in this town is truly astounding," she added. Then she grabbed the pen and the yellow legal pad from the briefcase. "Tell me what happened, Mr. Matthews."

"I was robbed," Matthews said.

She looked annoyed. "I know *that*. What I want to know is whether you can identify McBride."

"I've never seen him except for a few minutes when he and the other fellow were wrapped up together on the sidewalk. Even then I didn't get a good look at him. And I never saw a photo spread or a lineup or anything like that." For emphasis, he added: "The first time I'm going to get a really good look at him is when I take the stand."

CHAPTER 33

Fifteen minutes later, Matthews sat in the front of the courtroom beside Kevin Chalk, the man who was on the ground with McBride. McBride and his attorney, Jon Bennett, were seated at the defense table. Bennett was bald, with a sallow complexion and lanky arms and legs. He wore wire-rim glasses, which he constantly adjusted with his long-fingered, big-knuckled hands.

Gahagan placed her briefcase on the prosecutor's table as though it was a Brink's truck carrying some priceless cargo. Matthews knew what was really in it—practically nothing. So did Bennett, Matthews assumed.

Bennett moved for a rule on witnesses. The prosecutor turned and signaled for Matthews. Chalk was escorted outside to wait his turn to testify. Matthews raised his right hand, took the oath, and sat in the witness box.

"Would you please state your name for the record?" asked Gahagan.

"Sean Matthews."

Bennett propped a hand under his chin and studied Matthews. Matthews could feel the stare, focusing on his hair, his face, his clothes, and his posture. The defense attorney's eyes were cold and detached behind the wire-rim glasses and his lips pursed in a slight smile as he evaluated the witness.

Gahagan began the questioning. "Let me draw your attention to the third of September. Do you recall where you were that evening?"

"I was at a restaurant called Clippers, having dinner."

"And is Clippers located in the confines of Columbia Bay?"

"It is."

"Were you alone?"

"No. I was with a friend from Virginia."

"Move on, counselor," instructed the judge.

Gahagan looked at her notes. "How did you pay for the meal?"

"In cash. It was $140. I remember peeling off seven $20 bills."

Matthews looked at the defense table. Bennett's head was down. He was scribbling. Matthews wondered whether he was taking notes about the case or about something else. During a case, Matthews himself often lost focus and wrote notes to himself about other things. Multitasking with other people's lives, he thought wryly.

Matthews' eyes wandered to the defendant. It was the first time he had had a really good look at him. A shock ran through his body.

Bennett raised his head, like an animal alerting on a scent. Then he put his head back down. He was no longer scribbling.

"How much cash did you have with you that evening?"

"Several hundred dollars," Matthews replied.

Bennett removed his glasses. "Can the witness be more specific?" he asked, loudly and emphatically. "A wad of cash was found in the vicinity where my client was accosted. If Mr. Matthews is going to testify the money recovered belonged to him, I'd like to know the exact amount of cash he was carrying."

Matthews replied, "I had over $2,000 in various denominations."

"Why were you carrying so much cash?" asked the prosecutor.

"When I'm not practicing law, I collect art and antiques. I planned to do some antiquing the next day. Merchants, generally speaking, prefer cash. They don't like plastic, and only a few will take a check."

"What happened next?" asked Gahagan.

"We left the restaurant. When we got outside, I sensed something. It was as though a third person had joined us."

"Did you see anyone?"

"Not at first. We were just walking. The block was deserted. I glanced back and saw someone in the shadows. I recall taking the hand of my dinner date and stepping into the street. I had a premonition. I wanted to get out of there."

"Then what happened?"

"The robber spoke to us," Matthews said. "He was walking directly behind us. 'Sean, Jane,' he said. He knew our names. 'Don't turn around. Keep walking. If you turn around, I'm going to kill you.' He said he had a gun."

"What did you do?"

Matthews cleared his throat. "He instructed me to reach into my pocket, remove my money and to hand it to him. So I took the money out of my pocket and held it up." Matthews imitated removing the cash.

From the corner of his eye, he caught McBride sneering. Matthews rubbed one hand down his trouser leg, which was shaking uncontrollably.

"He grabbed the money out of my hand. He demanded my wallet and I gave it to him. Then things got quiet and I turned around. He was gone. I started yelling for help as loud as I could.

"A bunch of people appeared. I pointed in the direction the robber must've run. A voice came from that direction and yelled, 'I've got him.' We ran in that direction, rounded the corner, and saw two men on the ground. It looked like one had tackled the other."

Gahagan walked over to the evidence table and picked up the photos of the contents of Matthews' wallet and the money.

Bennett stood. "Photocopies were taken and the evidence returned to Mr. Matthews," he said. "We'll stipulate as to the wallet, its contents and the money collected at the scene."

"The exhibits are admitted," said the judge.

"Do you recognize either of those two men in the courtroom this morning?"

"Yes." Matthews pointed at McBride. The tremor had moved to his finger.

"I ask the court to note the witness has identified the defendant, Mr. McBride."

"So noted," the judge said.

Gahagan sat down. "No further questions."

Bennett approached, placed his hand on the witness box, and stared at Matthews like an entomologist studying an insect in a jar. "You never actually saw the robber at the time you handed him your money or wallet, did you?"

"That's correct," Matthews said. "He told us not to turn around."

"In fact, Mr. Matthews, the first time you saw the defendant, Stephen McBride, was when you ran over and saw him on the ground with another man, Kevin Chalk." Bennett glanced down at his notepad.

Matthews' instincts told him to just go ahead and answer, "Yes." But he answered truthfully.

"No, that's not correct."

"Are you saying you saw my client earlier, Mr. Matthews?" Bennett's voice was devoid of emotion. He had sensed it when Matthews recognized McBride a few minutes earlier.

Matthews looked at Gahagan.

"Don't look at the prosecutor," Bennett said softly, but firmly. "She's not going to tell you what to say. Just answer the question."

"Yes," Matthews said. Anticipating the next question, he added, "At the restaurant."

"Prior to the robbery?"

"That's right. I remember seeing him drinking at the bar, when I was paying the bill." He remembered asking about how Hutton wanted to pay the bill. He recollected seeing a couple of guys seated at the bar with an empty barstool between them.

"Was my client alone or with someone else?"

"He was alone, as far as I could tell," Matthews said.

"Do you recall if he was drinking or eating, Mr. Matthews?"

"I think he had a glass in front of him."

Bennett recalibrated. No need to risk spoiling it. Enough had been placed in the record. "No further questions," he said. And Matthews could be excused, Bennett said. He had no intention of recalling the witness.

As he headed for a seat, Matthews noticed Katz in the back of the courtroom. He smiled weakly. Katz gave a courteous wave. After all was said and done, Katz had acquiesced to Matthews' request and left McCarthy to grapple with the BOM.

CHAPTER 34

While the trial progressed in Columbia Bay, the conference room in the U.S. Attorney's office filled to capacity. McCarthy sat at the center of the table, with senior prosecutors seated to his left and right. Three black leather seats on the opposite side of the table were empty. Junior attorneys and support staff ringed the room, as though in attendance at a sold-out concert.

When the Bank of Magellan first learned about the federal investigation, it sent Hutton around the country to offer settlements with the families of each of the victims. No one accepted. Instead, the families turned to the U.S. Attorney's Office to seek justice for their losses.

Utilizing resources from the Treasury Department's antiterrorism office and attorneys detailed from the Department of Homeland Security, the attorneys slowly, painstakingly and methodically built an ironclad case against BOM.

"Miss Hutton is here," announced a receptionist.

No one expected a fight. Hutton did not take cases to trial; she settled them. Her work was in boardrooms, not courtrooms. She kept a checkbook in her briefcase, not a legal pad. Her mindset had nothing to do with evidence beyond a reasonable doubt. It was about the impact of adverse publicity upon the corporate bottom line.

"Show her in," said McCarthy. He texted Lin, seated somewhere in the room: "Showtime!" He did not stand when Hutton entered. He wanted to play tough, make her sweat. Today's negotiation would be cold and impersonal.

Hutton breezed in, cool and confident in a dark blue suit, white silk blouse with a deep V-collar, a single strand of pearls around her neck, and matching drop earrings. She did not extend her hand, dispensing with formalities and taking the seat opposite McCarthy. Her associates sat on either side of her, suits without expression.

Hutton had studied McCarthy and concluded he was a weak negotiator. He previously worked for Abe Lowenstein in Congress, where people were fawning and obsequious to a fault. Legislators and key staff mistook the deference of others as personal strength. Hutton saw it differently. Take away the power of the office, and these people were feeble and fragile.

Hutton shifted her chair back slightly. "You're lucky," she said.

"And why is that?" he asked.

"Because I have instructions from my client to avert publicity in this case. That means one thing. Settle. I'm not here to threaten to go to trial." She shook her head and laughed. "Name your price. My client wants to cut a deal." She tucked a loose strand of hair behind her ear and surveyed the testosterone-filled room. "What'll it be, boys?"

"Eight," he said after a moment's hesitation. "Eight hundred million dollars." It sounded like someone wagering a bet, someone who did not know how to gamble.

People around the table looked at one another. Without speaking, they all asked the same questions. Where did that number come from? Was it too high? Too low? The purpose of this meeting was not to agree to a specified payment. And wasn't Mac supposed to pursue an admission to criminal wrongdoing? What was going on?

"Eight hundred million," Hutton repeated. "That is a hell of a lot of money, Mr. McCarthy."

Hutton had actually expected something in the billions. She was authorized to go that high and was prepared to do so. But he had given her an opening and she was going to take full advantage of it.

"Your client's actions are egregious," he said, as though an explanation were required. "Magellan has to be taught a lesson. Each death was an affront to our flag and to our nation."

Hutton hid a smirk. Save that kind of rhetoric for a jury, she thought to herself. Of course, truth be told, she too considered Magellan despicable, but this man was such a horse's ass. She rose and ran a hand down the front of her skirt, smoothing the fabric. Then she extended a hand.

McCarthy rose unsteadily and hesitantly extended his hand.

"As well as an admission to the criminal complaint," said a woman seated in one of the chairs ringing the room. Everyone turned. It was Lin.

Hutton turned. "I'm sorry," she laughed. "I think you're a little late. We have an agreement. You can't add terms and conditions at this point."

McCarthy flushed. He put his hand down. "No, not a final agreement," he said, appearing confused. "Nothing is signed. We still have to work out the details." He sat back down.

Hutton assessed the situation. She may have saved her client a ton of money and had room to up the ante. But no, she told herself. She was entitled to have a little fun. Plus, all the risk seemed to be on the other side.

"I've accepted an $800 million settlement without a fight," she said. "The size of the settlement is an admission of wrongdoing in and of itself, isn't it? I'm not going to let you pull it back, seek even more money, and attach additional strings." Thank God the client was not in the room, she thought. They would be shitting bricks.

"I'm afraid there's some sort of disconnect here," said McCarthy. He sat seemingly paralyzed in his chair. "We should stop now and pick up this discussion later."

Hutton stared him down. "I'm not leaving until we sign a memo of understanding to settle for the agreed-upon amount. We have a deal. I expect you to honor it."

Rather than responding to Hutton, conferring with the staff, and restoring order to the negotiations, McCarthy got up and walked out of the room. Lin trailed a safe distance behind him. Hutton sat back easily and confidently with the air of someone who was in no rush to go anywhere.

"What's that all about?" whispered one of the attorneys. "Eight hundred million. Where did that come from?"

The room erupted into a cacophony of sound, as though the combustion in the room had ignited a flurry of vocal opinion, judgment, recrimination, and speculation. Everyone had something to say, and nobody agreed about anything, save for the fact that McCarthy had blown it.

**

McCarthy closed the door to his office. He stood in the center of the small square room and exhaled. An instant later, there was a knock on the door. He opened it, Lin walked in, and he closed the door behind her. "How'd I do?" he asked.

"Half the people in the room think you're totally incompetent and the other half think you're just uncharacteristically unprepared," she said. "No one thinks highly of your performance." Then, after a pause, she said, "So I'd say you did great."

They shared conspiratorial smiles.

Their efforts over the past two days failed to uncover the rationale for Landry's insistence on a swift settlement. If Landry was hiding someone or something, they could not figure out who or what it was, and they had scoured the file. In order to give them more time, McCarthy promised Lin that he would ad lib it when Hutton came to the office, and his improvisation amounted to a display of feigned ineptitude.

"I wonder if Landry's going to figure out this was nothing more than a ruse," McCarthy said.

"Not if I have anything to do with it," Lin said. "I'll make another trip to his office to reinforce the notion that you're out of your depth," she said.

He nodded his concurrence.

"Maybe Landry will lead us to the answer," she speculated. "You know what they say: the self-righteous self-immolate. Maybe Landry will fall apart and reveal what he's hiding."

"Maybe," McCarthy replied.

Lin left. McCarthy remained standing in the center of the office. He closed his eyes before returning to the conference room to suffer the consternation of his peers and the ridicule of Hutton and her colleagues.

CHAPTER 35

Back in Columbia Bay, Chalk followed Matthews to the stand. He testified that McBride ran into him while running around a corner at a high rate of speed, throwing both of them to the ground. The defense countered by suggesting it was the other way around, namely that Chalk ran into McBride.

The prosecution then rested.

Bennett opened the defense by calling the bartender from Clippers, who did not remember serving Stephen McBride. Then Bennett called six patrons who had been seated in the dining room. They remembered Matthews and Hutton, but not McBride. A bookkeeper testified that everyone used credit that night to pay their bills, except for Matthews. No credit or debit card was in the name of Stephen McBride.

Next was Paul Penn, who worked at the Port of Charleston. He testified he had been with McBride earlier in the evening discussing a business venture.

"What sort of business venture?" asked Bennett.

"It involves a treatment center for children in the southern states who suffer from a rare form of eye cancer," Penn said.

"McBride's a potential investor?"

"Yes, sir," replied Penn. "He's thinking of investing twenty-five percent. I don't have enough to make it happen alone. His participation is critical to our success."

On cross-examination, Gahagan showed the alibi was not airtight. According to Penn's testimony, there was enough time for McBride to get across town, drop into the bar, spot a patron with a wad of cash, and rob him. To Katz, listening in the back of the courtroom, that actually made the testimony more credible, since the best alibi is one that leaves room for a little seepage.

After Penn testified, Bennett called his client to the stand.

"You've heard the evidence presented against you today?" Bennett asked McBride.

"I have."

"Did you rob Sean Matthews that night?"

"I did not."

"Where were you?"

"I was with a friend discussing a business transaction."

"That was Mr. Penn?"

Gahagan objected. "Leading." Given the preceding testimony, it was a silly objection. Nonetheless, the judge sustained it. And Bennett took advantage of it.

"Do you recall who the man was?" he asked.

"Paul Penn," McBride replied.

"You're sure?" Bennett asked.

Everyone in the courtroom broke into laughter, including the judge.

"And what were you discussing with Paul Penn?"

"Just a small business matter," McBride said humbly.

"What kind of transaction?" Bennett asked.

Gahagan wanted to object. The question had been asked and answered. But the laughter that followed her last objection constrained her.

"He wants to bring a clinic to Columbia Bay," McBride said. "There's an abnormal number of adolescent children who suffer from a unique form of eye cancer in South Carolina and Georgia. Penn's dream is to bring relief to those children and their families. I plan to help him."

Bennett did not have to ask McBride whether he also loved dogs.

"How long did your meeting last?"

"Less than an hour."

"And what did you do then?"

"I headed home to Columbia Bay."

"And did you in fact go home?" Bennett asked.

"No," replied McBride.

"Why not?"

"I got a call from another friend," McBride explained. "Dan Robinson. He was having a problem with his mom. About putting her into a nursing home. He knew my mom had passed recently, and that she had spent her final months in a nursing home. He wanted to get some ideas on how to proceed."

"Did the two of you meet?"

"No," McBride said. "I never made it."

"Why was that?" asked Bennett.

"I had the misfortune of running into Mr. Chalk soon after I got out of the car."

Bennett turned to Gahagan. "Your witness," he said.

Gahagan tried her best, but McBride employed a sophisticated parry and thrust and, in the end, she did no damage to his credibility.

"No redirect," Bennett said nonchalantly when she finished.

"Does the prosecution have any witnesses for rebuttal?" the judge asked Gahagan, assuming Bennett had rested his case.

"Excuse me, your honor," Bennett said in an apologetic tone. "The defense has one more witness."

Watching in the back of the courtroom, Katz rubbed his chin. To put a witness on the stand *after* the defendant bordered on malfeasance, he thought to himself. People lie in court. A defendant can spot the lies and adjust his story correctly, since he's in the room. A witness sequestered during the testimony of other witnesses cannot do the same. There was no time to edit the story to fit the narrative presented in the courtroom.

"The defense calls Dan Robinson," Bennett said. A deputy went into the witness room and called Robinson's name. A slight, smiling man emerged and took the stand and was sworn.

"Do you recall where you were on the evening of Tuesday, September third?" Bennett asked Robinson.

"Yes, I was at a restaurant called Dunnigan's."

"What were you doing there?"

"Waiting for Steve McBride. I had asked him to join me, to give me some advice about a family problem I was having."

"What sort of problem?"

"Putting my mom in a nursing home."

"Did Mr. McBride show up?" Bennett asked.

"No. I waited nearly an hour. He's one of those guys who's always there for you. So I was surprised when he didn't show. Eventually, I left."

"Did you try to call him?"

"No, I just figured something had come up and he was busy. Later, I heard Steve had been arrested for robbery. I couldn't believe it."

"Thank you. No further questions." Short, sweet, and effective, Matthews thought, marveling at the mastery of the defense.

"I thank the court," Bennett said. "I have no further questions for this witness. The defense rests."

Gahagan searched her notes. She could ill afford to let the case end like this. She needed something. But after a painful minute of flipping pages in her legal pad, she looked up and said, "No further questions, your honor." The judge, unwilling to throw Gahagan a lifeline, did not ask any questions either.

Both parties rested. The judge recessed. She asked everyone to stay close by. She wanted to review the evidence and intended to render a verdict by evening.

**

It took less than an hour for Steve McBride to be acquitted. Immediately after the judge announced her decision, Bennett moved to expunge the record and seal the file.

Matthews and Katz walked across town after they heard the news. Matthews wanted to create a physical distance between himself and the courthouse. As dusk fell, they walked and talked. Sometime around 9 p.m., they separated and Katz took an Uber to the airport.

Matthews returned to his room. He would stay the night in Columbia Bay. He needed to take care of one bit of unfinished business before he departed for Washington the next morning.

As he was waiting to board his flight back to Washington, Katz pulled out his phone to check messages. He had not glanced at the phone all day. The mailbox was filled with texts and emails complaining about McCarthy's performance. Katz focused on one from Lin, which recited a line he thought was from Shakespeare's *Hamlet*:

"There's special providence in the fall of a sparrow."

CHAPTER 36

At 9 a.m. Friday morning, the 13th, as the fog lifted, a speedboat greeted a barge on the Potomac River south of the Wilson Bridge. As it approached, the new members of the crew grew apprehensive, but not the veterans. Not only were they expecting the speedboat, they were counting on it.

As the boat came along the starboard side, two men boarded the barge and inspected the cargo. The crew, including Morelli, dutifully moved to the speedboat. The barge continued upriver.

A moment later, Morelli texted Stone.

"Barge boarded. Speedboat headed to the pier near King Street."

Seated in an unmarked cruiser in the parking lot under the Wilson Bridge at Jones Point, Stone kept her eyes on the blinking light of a monitor in her hand. The light indicated the location of the crates containing the tracking devices. She looked up and glanced at the speedboat cutting across the water a quarter mile directly in front of her.

Her eyes shifted to the monitor as she noticed the light blinking directly beneath the Wilson Bridge.

Stone got out of the car and walked to the edge of the river. She could not see the barge. She looked to her right, then to her left. She returned to the car and looked at the tracking device. The barge was still parked directly beneath the bridge. She went back to the edge of the water and stared at the bridge, at the tarp that stretched from the top of the bridge down to the water's edge with the word PASHA displayed on it in big white letters.

Ten minutes later, the barge emerged and began its slow journey toward the waterfront. The monitor now displayed two lights. One light moved with the barge while the other light remained stationary beneath the bridge.

"Where is the barge now?" a voice barked over a walkie-talkie. It was a District undercover police officer she had alerted about the possible delivery of narcotics.

"It's just passed under the bridge," she replied. "Do you have your people positioned along the wharf?"

A muffled response came over the walkie-talkie. Undercover agents were in position, undetected among the hardhats in the work zone.

"The barge is approaching the shoreline," she was told fifteen minutes later by the undercover agent. "We'll wait to see who moves in and removes the materials from that barge. If there's anything suspicious, we'll strike."

Within an hour, it was evident there was not going to be any drug bust. The crates were offloaded at the construction site and pried open discreetly. A tracking device was found cradled among boxes of fancy Mexican tiles.

A search with sniffer dogs also found nothing.

"What the hell went wrong?" someone asked. "There has to be a reason the speedboat approached the barges and the crew disembarked. If it's not drugs, what is it?"

Shortly thereafter, the walkie-talkies went silent and the undercover operation disbanded. Stone was neither disappointed nor surprised. She drove from Jones Point to the Alexandria waterfront off King Street to pick up Morelli.

"Any luck in the District?" he asked as he got into her unmarked cruiser.

"Just construction stuff," she replied.

"I don't get it," he said, after a long silence. "I can't understand what went wrong."

"Neither could anyone else," Stone said, referring to the undercover agents in the District who had anticipated a big payday.

She drove back to Jones Point and parked at the end of the lot, the hood of her vehicle overlooking the Potomac with the Wilson Bridge off to the right.

"Some of the crates were taken off the barge at the Wilson Bridge," she said, looking out at the tarp flapping in the breeze. "One of the bugs is in those crates." She turned to Morelli. "The drugs never go into the District. The distribution point is right there."

"Are you sure?" Morelli asked, his surprise at her analysis evident.

"No question about it," she answered.

"That's incredible," Morelli said. "It's right under our noses."

"Right under truck tires and automobile frames, to be precise," Stone said.

In her mind's eye, Stone could see drugs carted off the barge before the innocent cargo chugged upriver. The crates could be lifted onto the bridge at night and loaded into vehicles. Some of those vehicles would take I-295 into the city. Others would head into the Maryland suburbs: Prince George's County, then up to Montgomery County and Columbia. Still others would head in the opposite direction to Virginia: into Alexandria, along Route 1 and I-95, across Fairfax, up into Loudoun and down into Prince William County, blanketing the entire metropolitan area from one central drop spot beneath the Wilson Bridge.

A drug drop spot at the very edge of the imaginary diamond that formed the District of Columbia's borders, as she saw it. Never actually landing on terra firma and risking detection by drug enforcement officers patrolling the I-95 corridor.

"What are you going to do about it?" he asked.

"All we have to do is station officers along the bike path across the bridge and wait for the pick-up vehicles to arrive," she explained. "We'll seal off either end of the bridge and nab them in the middle of the operation."

"That sounds easy enough," he said.

She nodded. The way she saw it, there was another reason the drug syndicate was shipping its wares along the river. It was easy to flush away the evidence. The river was like one big commode. If vice and narcotics agents showed up on the bridge, all the dealers had to do was heave their cargo over the side.

"I've only got one more question," Morelli said. "Are we sure this is about drugs?" He furrowed his brow. "I saw those crates loaded down at Hampton Roads. They were super big and heavy as elephants. It got me wondering. Could these guys be shipping that amount of drugs at one time?"

"What else could it be?" asked Stone.

Morelli shrugged. "I don't know. But a couple of those containers could have held a Civil War cannon."

CHAPTER 37

At around 10 a.m., Matthews drove to McBride's home, located on a quiet cul-de-sac in Columbia Bay filled with contemporary homes set back on manicured lawns. McBride was standing on the front porch reading something on his phone.

Matthews parked and walked up a flagstone path to the house. He stopped at the base of the porch. "I dropped by to apologize," he said contritely.

"What?" McBride asked.

Matthews was uncertain whether McBride heard him the first time and was taking sinister delight in making him repeat the words. Regardless, he was in the wrong. "I dropped by to apologize," he said.

"No need to," McBride replied. "You believed I was guilty. I can't fault a man for holding to his principles."

Matthews smiled uncomfortably. Grace under fire, or so he wanted to believe.

"I don't think you're a malicious man or one who took pride in dragging my character through the mud," McBride continued. If those words were intended to console Matthews, they only made him feel worse. McBride walked down from the porch to the walkway with the air of a king descending a throne to acknowledge a commoner.

They shook hands. They looked at one another. There was nothing more to say. Matthews nodded and turned toward his car. When Matthews was halfway down the walkway, McBride asked, "By the way, Sean, did you need any formal clothes or did the casual attire suffice?"

A sprinkler system turned on at that instant, spraying water across the manicured lawn with the precision of a machine gun. McBride turned, walked back up the steps to the porch and through the front door, which closed quietly behind him. Matthews stood frozen on the walkway, the water striking his pant legs from the knee down as it moved across the lawn.

**

An hour later, Matthews called Hutton. No one answered. He left a message.

"Jane, I'm sorry to bother you. And I know I've been a real shit. But that's not why I'm calling." His voice shook. "You probably haven't heard, but Steve McBride was acquitted of the robbery charges. So I met with him this morning to apologize for falsely identifying him. As we parted, he said, 'By the way, Sean, did you buy any formal clothes at Columbia Bay or did the casual attire suffice?' Or something like that."

Matthews was standing in the sterile area of the airport, having already passed through the security checkpoint. "That's what we were discussing in the restaurant that night," he continued. "It's the only place he could have heard it. Can you believe it? He *was* the one who robbed me, who robbed us." Matthews' heart was racing. "I just thought you'd want to know."

If there was a bottle of bourbon or a container of painkillers handy, he might have grabbed them. Instead, he sat down, gripping the phone in one hand and his carry-on bag in the other, and waited to board the flight to Washington.

When he landed an hour later, he called an Uber to take him to his apartment on H Street. He spent the day in seclusion trying to process the morning's revelation. The court had been misled and justice had been perverted. He had been victimized twice, once by McBride and once by the system. A part of him wanted to turn in his license and become a victims' rights advocate.

CHAPTER 38

Katz called the BOM team to his office a little after noontime. He was furious. He was gone one day and the case was in tatters. Opposing counsel claimed a settlement had been reached. *The Washington Post* was reporting that criminal charges would not be filed against BOM. Angry complainants quoted in the story demanded an explanation. Office morale flagged. Accusatory fingers pointed to McCarthy, along with claims of incompetence bordering on malfeasance.

"All you had to do was set the broad parameters for settlement," Katz said, directing his ire at everyone in the room. "You should have anticipated they might go to endgame, and you should have been prepared." He swept his hand over his head, his fingers combing through his wiry hair. "Being prepared didn't mean throwing out numbers and getting yourself boxed into a corner."

As he spoke, Katz studied the faces in the room. He paid particularly close attention to McCarthy, who kept his head down, except one time when he looked up at Lin, who returned his gaze with an inscrutable expression.

After giving the staff a public flogging, Katz got down to business.

"We're going to pull this case back on the rails," he said. "First, we're going to increase the terms of settlement to over a billion dollars. We're not going for a paltry $800 million, not while I'm in charge. This case cries out for a penalty that will stun every mercenary in the world.

"Second, we're going to get a plea to a criminal charge. If there's not a plea to a criminal charge, we are taking this case to trial. We are going to pummel the other side with everything we've got."

First one person clapped. Then the entire room broke into applause. It was deafening.

Katz put up his hand. "You've had one hell of a week. It's Friday, so, as soon as your docket is clear, give yourselves a long weekend. On Monday, we'll set up another conference with Jane Hutton." Then he pointed at McCarthy. "In my office, in five minutes."

**

Katz nodded for McCarthy to sit in one of the four chairs at a small conference table against the window at the far end of the office. He remained seated at his desk. He called Lin. "Are you available to join us?" He remained silent until Lin joined them. She sat next to McCarthy.

Katz closed the door and returned to his swivel chair, which he turned to them, putting an elbow on his desk and crossing his legs. McCarthy fidgeted in his chair. Lin remained motionless.

"I caught your conspiratorial glance at one another a few minutes ago," Katz said. Then, to Lin, he added, "I saw it in your face the other night, when you had me over for dinner. You wanted to tell me something. And yesterday you sent me a message with a line from Shakespeare that I could only interpret to mean that Mac's meltdown had some higher meaning."

McCarthy looked questioningly at Lin. "Hamlet," she whispered. He nodded approvingly.

"The way you two act makes me wonder whether this entire debacle was deliberate," Katz said. He studied their faces, which broke into smiles. "So you *did* do this on purpose," he said. "What the hell for?"

McCarthy and Lin gushed information. McCarthy described the meeting in Lowenstein's office and Landry's inexplicable interest in a settlement. He also revealed the sting operation, as best as he understood it. Lin shared details of her trip to Landry's headquarters in Crystal City and the model of the Wilson Bridge. They both explained the subsequent rendezvous with Stone, Reese, and Morelli and the issuance of the warrant. McCarthy said he had not heard back from Stone but would follow up later in the day.

Finally, McCarthy shared the phone conversation that took place with Landry on Thursday morning. "He told me Hutton was going to offer a settlement. He acted as though it was all set. There was no way I was going to accommodate him, even if it meant making a fool of myself."

Katz listened intently. When they finished, he showed no compassion. "That is the most twisted logic I've ever heard. You had inside information that a settlement was in the offing, yet you deliberately ignored capitalizing on it. I'll admit there are some oddities about this case, but nothing justified jeopardizing a settlement."

Yet, he thought to himself, Mac risked his reputation because his instincts told him to do so. That meant something. He shook his head, then smiled as his two colleagues squirmed. "I don't know what I'm going to do with the two of you."

"Let us keep digging," Lin entreated, relieved. "There's an explanation for why Landry wanted the case to settle, and we think it's connected to whatever's going on along the Potomac and at the Wilson Bridge."

"Be my guest," Katz said. "But I'm going to call Hutton back to the office and bring the BOM case to a conclusion."

**

After they left, Katz turned to face the window so no one entering could see the expression on his face. His decision to go to Columbia Bay was less about consoling Matthews than about giving McCarthy and Lin room to operate unimpeded by his presence. Now he smiled, satisfied that his decision to follow his instincts had been the correct course of action. Mac's performance was unconventional, but Katz felt it was getting them closer to a successful outcome.

**

McCarthy and Lin sequestered themselves in a windowless room for the remainder of the day, surrounded by cardboard boxes with documents pertaining to the BOM case. McCarthy drank coffee and Lin sipped water as they silently examined interview transcripts, financial statements, notes, spreadsheets, and assorted investigatory materials.

"I didn't know Landry was an investigator in this case," Lin said as she reviewed notes of an interview conducted by the head of the antiterrorism unit.

"Early on," McCarthy acknowledged. He ran his hand through his hair. He decided it was time to share with Lin the information he had previously withheld from her.

"Senator Lowenstein told me that Landry was offered information by a suspect in our case in exchange for a get-out-of-jail card from the

141

BOM prosecution. Landry accepted the offer. That's why he dropped out of the BOM case."

"Thanks for sharing," Lin said sarcastically, disgusted by McCarthy's disingenuous antics. "Were you ever going to reveal that little tidbit of information if I hadn't stumbled upon it on my own?"

McCarthy bowed his head apologetically.

"You always operate like this," Lin castigated him. "I'm not angry, just disappointed. If it was someone else, they'd probably stop working with you. It's no way to build trust, you know."

Then she quickly put her disappointment aside and refocused on the matter at hand. "If all of that's true," she said, "then Landry encouraged you to settle BOM because he's afraid a prolonged investigation will reveal his source. He doesn't want anything to jeopardize his sting operation."

"Exactly," McCarthy replied, grateful that Lin was willing to overlook his lack of frankness with her. "If we can pinpoint what Landry was working on before he left – who he interviewed, which files he reviewed, things like that – then we can identify the suspect."

Lin nodded in agreement.

"Listen," McCarthy said contritely, "I'm sorry about holding back information. I suggested to Senator Lowenstein tracking down the suspect, but he discouraged me. That's no excuse for not telling you, but maybe it influenced my thinking."

Lin just looked at him, unmoved. He added, "You're right, what you said a minute ago. I do have a nasty habit of sharing only pieces of information with other people while keeping the entire picture to myself. It's just the way I'm wired. I'll try to do better from this point forward. I'm sorry."

Lin softened. "Apology accepted," she said. "Let's get to work."

Afternoon turned into evening and evening into night. They perused files in the windowless room oblivious to time. Their only respite was to read an email from Stone about the results of the search warrant.

CHAPTER 39

At about 10 p.m., Matthews left his apartment and drove to his office in Alexandria. He took a route along the Anacostia River and across the Wilson Bridge. The moon, nearly full, led his way.

Sidewalks in Old Town swelled with bar-hoppers and foodies, roaming the streets on this Friday the 13th.

Matthews parked in the alley. The moon created elongated shadows across the gravel parking lot. He ascended the wooden stairs to the back entrance of the office.

The suite smelled old and musty as he entered. The moon cast rays of light through the blinds and across the carpet. He went to his office, flipped on the light switch, and sat at his desk facing a pile of papers.

A manila file labeled "Pasha Industries" sat on a corner of the desk. Matthews grabbed the file and leafed through it, studying memos, letters, and photographs. Prolokov must have left it behind, he concluded. The contents bore no relation to the construction business. Some of the correspondence was in Cyrillic type. Photos of military hardware were clearly marked in English. A Russian-made surface-to-air missile system was labeled "SA-11." Another was labeled "Buk," and a third "Gadfly."

SA-11 seemed vaguely familiar. Matthews had read something about the downing of a commercial jetliner, hadn't he? And Gadfly. Where had he seen that word before? Slowly his thoughts crystalized as though he was looking at a hologram.

The material in the file alarmed him. It included information about fragmented warheads, proximity fuses, forty-six pounds of explosives per missile, detonation capability one hundred feet from the target, shrapnel clouds.

Suddenly, there was a noise. Matthews looked up, startled. Dark forms hovered over him.

"Boris," Matthews started. "What the hell are you doing here?" He tried to act casual. He looked at the dense form beside Prolokov.

"We did not expect to see you here so late," Prolokov said. He moved around the desk. The file was still open. Matthews tried to ignore the file, to no avail.

The Russian pondered the situation for a long minute. "You understand?" he asked, pointing at the photo of the surface-to-air missile.

Matthews tried to look more confused than he was, but unfortunately he now understood only too well. "I'm not sure what you're talking about," he answered. His voice cracked. "I just opened the file. I really haven't studied its contents."

Matthews frantically looked for an object to use as a weapon. He grabbed his desk phone and hit the speed dial. "Look," he cried, "I don't know what's going on. I'm not going to say anything."

"I am very sorry, Sean," Prolokov said. He frowned sadly. "I tried to keep this information from you, but now you know."

Suddenly a serrated blade glittered in front of Matthews, whose eyes opened wide in alarm. The blade plunged into his neck below the Adam's apple and across the flesh like a razor ripping through paper.

**

Prolokov appeared at the back door of the law office. He pulled a handkerchief from his pocket and wiped his brow. He lit a cigarette and smoked it slowly. Finally he flicked it off the porch onto the gravel driveway. He descended the stairs and snuffed out the cigarette with his heel.

Around the corner, a car sat against the curb, a sole figure behind the wheel, his head down. The moon glow cast eerie shadows up and down the street. The only sound was the buzz of a streetlight standing like a sentry at the corner.

Prolokov pulled out his phone and punched in a number. "Come to the attorney's office," he said cryptically. "He has had an accident. You need to dispose of the body. Bring Alec. Burn the building to the ground. Do it quickly."

He put away the phone and went back inside. He stood looking at Matthews, jiggling change in his pocket. Regret replaced the sadness previously cast on his face.

**

Katz arrived at his place on Harvard Street before 11 p.m. Santana was waiting on the porch. In the distance, sirens sounded. Katz tilted his head in the direction of the cacophony of noise. "A full moon on Friday the 13th," he said. "What else would you expect?"

They went inside. Katz got a glass and a bottle of Green Hat gin out of the kitchen cabinets and poured a drink for Santana. He grabbed a Port City lager out of the refrigerator for himself. "This bachelor's life is killing me," he confided. "I've got dinner engagements every night for the next week. Tonight I had dinner with Suzie Marston."

Marston had been Katz's office manager during his years in private practice. She accompanied him to the U.S. Attorney's office, but decided within a year that retirement was more to her liking. The birth of a grandchild and a scare with a faulty cancer diagnosis had something to do with it.

"How's she doing?" Santana asked, smiling as he recalled fond memories of working with Marston when he was Katz's private investigator.

"She's happy," Katz said. "What's up with you?"

"The other day, when I told you about my surveilling Landry, I neglected to tell you something. In the course of my work, I saw Lin visit his headquarters in Crystal City."

Katz laughed. "Not to worry," he said. "I had a heart-to-heart with her and McCarthy earlier today." Then he shared the information they provided to him.

Santana was relieved.

Suddenly Katz's phone vibrated, then Santana's phone buzzed. They grabbed their devices simultaneously.

"Son of a bitch," Santana said, reading his text. "It's from Joey Cook. Sean Matthews' townhouse burned down tonight. I hope he's alright. Those sirens we heard must have been the fire engines responding to the scene."

Katz received the same message. He also noticed a call at 10:28. There was no accompanying message. He pressed the number. The phone rang without an answer. "I think Sean might have called me about an hour ago," he said. "I'm calling him back now, but there's no answer."

"Should we go over there?" Santana asked.

"I don't know what we could do to help," Katz said. "If there's a problem, he'll call back."

Santana received another text. It read:

BE AT YOUR PLACE IN 10 MINUTES.

"Good enough," said Santana. "I'm glad I checked in with you about Lin. Good thing we don't have to worry about her." He finished his gin, bid Katz a good night, and left. Katz turned off all his electronic devices and retired for the night. Between the trip to Columbia Bay and the BOM case, he was exhausted.

**

Landry sat in his car, which had not moved in an hour. Anxiously, he tapped the keyboard and typed a text message.

PICK-UP AT 1:30 PM TUES, SEPT. 17

He expected pushback on the other end since it was a daytime operation. All of the others had occurred in the middle of the night. But an instant later, he received a response of acquiescence. Good, he thought to himself. Things were going his way. Now he only had to bring the operation to endgame.

CHAPTER 40

Early Saturday morning, as night faded into day, the sun peeked over the eastern horizon and the moon turned translucent. A jogger edged along the trail at Jones Point. She stopped to catch her breath at an abutment facing the bridge at the river's edge and shuddered from the wind off the river. Looking out to the water, she saw something floating about twenty feet away. She squinted. She was sure it was a body bobbing face-down in the water.

In the distance, the Wilson Bridge, bathed in light, radiated early fall splendor. A huge tarp hanging from the span, inscribed with the insignia PASHA, flapped in the wind. The sound reverberated across the water.

The jogger turned and ran away from the bridge. As she did so, a blood-curdling scream suddenly echoed behind her. She looked over her shoulder. A child in a yellow parka was facing the water, staring right at the body bobbing in the water, screaming at the top of her lungs.

The woman saw a dog dragging a leash and a man running frantically toward the child and the dog. The man was dressed in a T-shirt and shorts.

"Amy," he hollered. "Amy, get over here right now!" He looked out on the water. Then he looked back at the girl and the dog, which had stopped protectively beside the girl. "And grab Bungee."

The jogger frowned. The man was probably going to take his daughter and dog and run back to the safety of his townhome and hide, probably in his wine cellar, she thought. He was not going to report it. He would let someone else handle the mess. Just like she was doing.

She pulled a phone from the pocket of her lightweight sweatshirt and dialed 911.

"Hello, I'm at Jones Point," she told the emergency operator calmly. "A body is floating in the water near the shoreline. Please send help right away."

She listened to the dispatcher on the other end. She turned, noticing the man was gone, along with the child and the dog. "No," she said, "I'm alone."

She waited for the police and EMTs to arrive. She gave a statement. Then she jogged toward home. Along the way, she stopped and threw up.

**

"Mo?"

Katz propped himself up on the side of the bed. He had just reactivated the phone before it rang. He was expecting to hear from Abby. Through the blinds, the blue and white colors of early dawn appeared.

It was Joey Cook, the town crier of the law enforcement community, broadcasting the latest news from his crib in the property room of the Alexandria Police Department.

"Sean Matthews is dead," Cook said. "His body was dumped near the Wilson Bridge. They found it earlier this morning."

Katz tried to process the information. He was silent for a long minute. "What happened?" he asked finally.

"The facts are sketchy," Cook said. "He was butchered pretty badly. And, like I texted last night, that shoebox of his that fronted as a law office was torched. I mean, there is nothing left. A very professional job."

Katz threw back the sheets. He turned and dropped his feet to the cold hardwood floor. Although he had a soft spot for Matthews, he knew the deceased attorney had probably earned the contempt of nearly everyone he'd represented. But it made no sense that one of Matthews' reprobate clients would do this to him.

"What are you thinking?" asked Cook.

"The same thing you are," Katz replied. "This wasn't a disgruntled client. It was something else." Then he asked, "Who's handling the investigation?"

"Stoner."

"Good choice."

Cook said nothing.

"Anything else?" asked Katz.

"The body was found off Jones Point. What was Matthews doing there? He didn't live down by the water. He had a little place off H Street in the District. It's strange.

"Someone lured Matthews to Jones Point and killed him, maybe a sexual liaison. Then they burned his office to the ground. I've seen cases where aggrieved lovers do crazy shit like that."

Katz was having none of it. "Let Stone investigate the case, Joey, before you start offering any wild theories about the case."

"Yeah, right," Cook said. "I'm going to miss him. Sean wasn't a bad guy, actually. I never told you this, but he took one for me back in the day."

"What do you mean, 'he took one for me back in the day'?"

"A couple of years ago," Cook explained, "I was running a scam in District Court, using praecipes to dispose of traffic cases and sneaking them past prosecutors and probation officers to the bench. I slipped one into a file he was handling. He was accused of tricking the prosecution, but, in reality, I was tricking him. He figured it out and gave me holy hell for setting him up, but he never reported me.

"In the end, I got demoted and ended up down here. If it hadn't been for Matthews, it would have been a lot worse. I would have been fired. Now I work in a dungeon, but at least I'm collecting a paycheck and I'll get my retirement. "

"You don't say," Katz said.

**

Ten minutes later, Katz's phone vibrated. It was Snowe texting. "Staying another week. Be good. Love you."

He texted back, "OK. Do what you have to do. Life is precious. Love you too." He didn't write anything about Matthews.

CHAPTER 41

Mid-morning, Stone surveyed the debris that was once Sean Matthews' office. It was reduced to a pile of smoldering rubbish. The small wood-framed building had ignited like a match, an arsonist's dream. Matthews had not complied with local fire regulations, so there were no sprinklers in the ceilings or fire alarms anywhere in the building. Not that it would have made a difference, the building having been doused in gasoline from the street entrance to the exit door that opened onto a rickety wooden staircase leading to the alley.

Earlier, Stone had been at Jones Point, where she had viewed Matthews' body being pulled from the water. She had interviewed the jogger who discovered the body; the woman had no evidence to provide and preferred being left out of the case. Stone had walked around the parking lot at Jones Point, studying the bollard the body had struck and the edge of the pier where the body had been thrown into the water.

The previous morning, she was tracking a shipment of drugs up the Potomac River. That investigation was now on the back burner as she dealt with a murder.

"What do you make of it?" asked Reese, who had accompanied her to the arson site.

"It doesn't add up," she said, staring at the ashes. "If they were going to torch the building, they should have left the body inside. Whoever murdered Matthews must have called someone else to burn the place down and get rid of the body. There must have been a miscommunication of some sort, resulting in the body being dropped at Jones Point."

"Why there, do you think?"

"I'm not sure," she replied. "Maybe it was the only place that came to mind."

Stone noticed a cigarette butt lying beside a dumpster at the edge of the parking lot. She summoned a member of the forensics team. "Pick up that cigarette and have it tested at the lab for DNA," she instructed. A drop of rain fell. "Do it quickly," she added, looking up at the menacing clouds cloaking the sky.

Then she summoned one of the officers on the scene. "Make sure every prospective witness is interviewed," she said. "Find out if there were any tenants in the apartment below the office. If so, interview them. Also, find out if any homeless people frequent this alley and find them too."

She turned to Reese. "When you get back to the office, check the court dockets in every jurisdiction. I want to know everyone with whom Matthews went to court in the past ninety days. I don't care whether it's a felony or a traffic offense. It's possible that a client held a grudge over the outcome of some case."

Reese promised to complete the task over the weekend.

Television crews were already assembled on the sidewalk. They had heard about Matthews' body being found. In everyone's mind, the fire and the murder were linked. Stone walked over to them. The reporters and cameramen formed a circle around her.

"What can you tell us at this time?" a reporter asked.

"I can tell you that every criminal makes mistakes," she said coldly. "It's only a matter of time before we find this murderer and arsonist."

"Do you have any leads?" asked another reporter.

She looked in the cameras. "Yes, we already have a few at this time but I'm not at liberty to share them. We'll bring the perpetrator of this heinous crime to justice," she said confidently.

**

Following the discovery of Matthews' body at Jones Point, news surfaced of the disappearance of a fisherman on the opposite bank of the Potomac River. Suddenly, the river banks were crawling with police from Alexandria, the District of Columbia, and Prince George's County.

Facing this unexpected turn of events, Landry concluded it was necessary to advance the date of his operation. Increased police scrutiny would inevitably lead to a search around and under the Wilson Bridge, most likely resulting in the discovery of the floating barge and the crates containing illegal arms. He concluded regretfully that the carefully choreographed plan to take down the terrorists on Constitution Day had to give way to these unforeseen developments.

"Listen up, people," he said to the team leaders summoned to the command center at 2 p.m. Saturday. "Cops from Virginia and Maryland are going to be all over the waterfront. As a result, I'm arranging to have the final cache of arms moved off the floating barge and transported to the warehouse.

"Our original plan was to take down the terrorist cell on the bridge. That's changed. Our current plan is to stage a massive sweep at the warehouse next Tuesday, the 17th. Any questions?"

A hand went up in the back of the room. It was the same woman who raised a question the previous week. "Like I asked before, why wait until next Tuesday? Doesn't it make more sense to use the resources of Alexandria and P.G. County to do a massive takedown now?"

Landry looked at her angrily. "This has been a special operation from the date of its inception," he replied. "We aren't going to reach out to other local or state officers, and we're not going to revise the date for busting the terrorist operation." He surveyed the room. "Any other questions?"

Another hand went up. "What about the weather?"

"It shouldn't be a problem if we move fast enough," Landry replied.

"So is this the end of Operation Open Sky?" someone asked. The inquiry seemed to be accompanied by a snicker.

Landry did not dignify the question with a reply.

*

The National Weather Service Storm Prediction Center had issued a weather warning shortly before Landry called the meeting. The warning was updated as he was speaking. Rainfall for the next two days was upgraded from "slight" to "enhanced." A squall line moving across the Ohio Valley was quickly migrating toward Washington. Air was increasingly unstable as a corridor of rain swept across West Virginia, driven by ferocious winds, with another line moving down from Pennsylvania toward western Maryland.

Before the meeting concluded, dark clouds filled the sky. Light rain was already hitting the windows. The forecast called for significantly worse conditions. Gale-force winds, fierce rain, and flooding threatened the DMV region from the mouth of the Chesapeake as far south as Hampton Roads. Meteorologists predicted 48 hours of torrential downpours before calm was restored in the atmosphere.

One storm formed from Shepherdstown, West Virginia, to Luray, Virginia. A smaller but equally intense system engulfed the area from Lansdowne to Clifton, Virginia, with warnings of tornadoes. Golf-ball-size hail was falling throughout Fauquier County and in northern Prince William County. The storms quickly formed a single front stretching from Gaithersburg, Maryland, all the way to the Marine base in Quantico, Virginia.

The threat existed that a derecho would hit the city by evening, like the one that hit Washington in 2012, packing 60-to-80-miles-per-hour winds, felling trees, dropping power lines, and creating havoc throughout the metropolitan area.

As fate would have it, the center of the storm was almost exactly where the Wilson Bridge was located.

Within thirty minutes after Landry's speech, rain fell in torrents. Winds grabbed anything that was loose – trash containers, recycling bins, newspaper boxes – and flung it on the sidewalks and the streets. Trash, leaves, and other debris were swept away by the flooding water overpowering sewers and drainage systems.

Landry's plan to remove the crates from the floating barge beneath the Wilson Bridge to the warehouse was also swept away like one more item in the storm's path. Until the storm passed, everything remained in abeyance. Search crews cancelled efforts to find the missing fisherman on the Maryland shore. The investigation at Jones Point where Matthews' butchered body was found similarly came to a stop.

**

The storm flung itself at the city. For the next 24 hours, Washington remained under a weather emergency. Conditions worsened by the hour. The entire metro area slowed to a virtual halt, like a body immobilized during surgery and clinging to life support.

CHAPTER 42

The storm had lost little of its intensity when Hutton appeared unannounced at the U.S. Attorney's office at 10 a.m. on Monday, the 16th.

A letter emailed from Katz to Stephens, Babcock & Brazier on Sunday recommended the resumption of settlement negotiations. A formal copy of the letter was mailed on Monday. Hutton did not wait for its delivery.

This morning, she was dressed casually in a yellow turtleneck sweater, black skirt, and black flats. Katz, who anticipated her return, had chosen to dress in an open-collar shirt, slacks, and blazer.

The two of them met alone in his office.

"I'm prepared to negotiate from a level playing field," she said. "My client's in a bad place and wants to get this over. You understand that, don't you?"

He did. Magellan had spent a small fortune preparing for trial, a trial they were likely to lose based on the evidence. Furthermore, the negative publicity surrounding the litigation had tanked the company's stock. All along, Hutton wanted one thing: to extricate her client from the specter of litigation.

"I've spent years on your side of the fence," Katz said. "I'm prepared to reach a just and equitable settlement."

Hutton knew Katz had been a shrewd defense attorney prior to becoming a federal prosecutor. He was a lawyer with steely nerves and crafty maneuvers who always had a trick up his sleeve. She could play around with McCarthy, but not with Katz. Plus, Matthews' murder had shaken her and she had lost some of her fight.

"I'm going to lay it on the table," Katz said. "One offer, non-negotiable. Take it or leave it. We're ready to go to trial if necessary, and, if we do, we'll prevail. The offer is $3.8 billion and an admission to the criminal complaint."

Hutton took a deep breath. "That's a long way from $800 million," she protested, although it was actually pretty close to her original expectation. A bit high, granted, but in the ballpark. The criminal charge was expected as well.

"We're locked and ready," Katz said. "By the time the trial is over, your client's name will be worthless and your reputation will be shredded." He did not sound boastful or threatening, only matter-of-fact. "Any chance at rehabilitating your corporate image will be gone forever."

She studied his face as she curled her lower lip and pressed her upper teeth against it. His face was calm. "I need to consult with my client," she said. "It's beyond the ceiling that I'm authorized to accept."

"I understand," Katz said. They stood and shook hands. Katz said she had until close of business Friday to accept or reject the offer.

As she prepared to leave, Hutton said, "I heard you went to Columbia Bay with Sean for the trial last week. That was a very nice gesture on your part."

Katz nodded. They had both avoided talking about Matthews, although he was on both of their minds. "I really debated about it before deciding to go," he said. "As things turned out, I'm glad I did. It was the last time I saw him. What happened to him was a horrible thing."

She lowered her eyes. "I agree. It's so sad." Then she raised her eyes to him and asked, "Have they made any progress in figuring out who might have done this to him? Probably a disgruntled client, so far as I can tell."

"Yeah, I don't know," he said. "It's being handled by the Alexandria police."

"Listen," she added. "Sean didn't know anything about my plans for meeting with McCarthy. I only told one person about my strategy and it wasn't him. Don't be angry that he didn't forewarn you."

Katz shook his head. "I wouldn't expect you to confide in him. And, if you had, I wouldn't expect him to share that confidence with me. So no bad feelings about it at all. But I am curious as to whom you informed about the settlement."

"One guess," she smiled slyly.

"Phil Landry."

"No way," she laughed heartily.

**

155

After Hutton left, Katz went to the windowless room where McCarthy and Lin remained holed up. "Any progress?" he asked.

"Slow but steady," McCarthy answered. "We're operating under the theory that Landry ceased working on BOM after turning a suspect into a confidential informant, and that the confidential informant played a role in setting up the sting operation at the Wilson Bridge."

"Go on," Katz said.

"We've identified all of the individuals Landry interviewed prior to his departure from the BOM investigation," Lin said. "They included a hedge fund operator, an attorney, a state politician in Norfolk, and a couple of businessmen. None of those individuals factored into the case as it evolved, either as witnesses or suspects. However, one of them might be connected to the sting operation."

Katz raised his eyebrows.

"Boris Prolokov," said Lin. "He runs a construction company currently working on the bridge. It's called Pasha. When I visited Landry in Crystal City, the model of the bridge had a paper towel draped over it, just like the tarp that hangs over the construction site."

McCarthy continued the narrative. "Prolokov was interviewed about arms shipments in the Middle East. His involvement was sketchy and he may have played a tangential role in moving the illegal arms financed by BOM that ultimately killed American soldiers in Afghanistan."

Katz sat down. The air conditioning system suddenly turned on and a stream of cold air rushed through a ceiling vent. The room was as cold as a freezer. He turned up his collar and crossed his arms over his chest.

Lin laughed and said, "It keeps us awake."

Katz smiled. "So what's your theory about Prolokov?"

"We think Prolokov concocted the terrorist plot in order to buy his freedom," McCarthy said. "I mean, think about it. He was about to be implicated in the BOM case by Landry, so he made a deal with Landry to buy his freedom."

Katz agreed that their theory held promise. "Go ahead and pursue every possible lead," he instructed them. He looked around the windowless walls and said, "There's a storm raging outside and it's getting fiercer by the minute. You both should pack up your computers and continue this from home."

**

Neither McCarthy nor Lin heeded Katz's advice. Instead, they continued working, oblivious to whatever was happening outside. They both sensed they were getting closer with every passing minute. As he surveyed their findings, McCarthy's eyes narrowed. "We need to inform Stone right away," he said.

CHAPTER 43

Stone drove through a driving rain in Crystal City to the access road at Reagan National Airport. She could get to the U.S. Attorney's office in 20 minutes. Lin said they had to meet right away. It sounded urgent.

She executed a sharp right and then looped left to get onto the southbound lanes of the G.W. Parkway. Stone had noticed a car following behind and checked her rearview mirror. Sure enough, a pair of headlights glowed behind her from a vehicle that had taken the same turn. It was not some secret route – cutting across the airport road to the parkway – but not a heavily traveled one either.

As she approached Old Town, she veered off onto West Abington Drive to parallel the parkway. At the intersection, she swung hard left onto Slaters Lane and then East Abington Drive so that she was now turned around and traveling in the northbound lane. The car's tires sliced through deep standing water from a drain clogged with debris and splashed water three feet into the air.

Through the rearview mirror, she saw headlights behind her executing the same series of turns.

Her phone, lying in the passenger seat, vibrated. She glanced at it. Reese had just sent an email. It would have to wait until later.

Stone accelerated, driving by Daingerfield Island to the right in the direction of the airport. Rain crashed against her windshield and she turned the wiper switch as high as it could go. As she approached the bridge over Four Mile Run, Stone swung right onto the concrete apron and stopped her car. She scooted across the front seat and exited the passenger-side door facing oncoming traffic, her hand on the grip of her firearm.

The car that had been behind her turned into the left-hand lane and accelerated. The night was black and the rain pounded against her face and body. She was unable to catch the license plate number. Stone raced around the car and, drenching wet, opened the door, jumped into the driver's seat, and put her vehicle in drive to pursue the other car.

Just then a group of cars swept by her like a flock of geese, forcing Stone to remain on the shoulder for critically important seconds.

She chose not to activate her siren. By the time she got onto the parkway, the chase was futile. The other vehicle had sped ahead and probably turned right at the 14th Street Bridge to enter D.C.

Stone drove all the way to Spout Run, where she turned around and headed back to Old Town Alexandria. Her heart was pounding and adrenaline coursed through her system. Who was following her, and why?

**

Thirty minutes later, Stone was seated in McCarthy's office. Her hair was mostly dry but untidy, like seaweed. Her shirt, pants, and boots were still wet.

McCarthy explained everything to her, beginning with his meeting in the Russell Senate Office Building and ending with his surmise, and Lin's, that Landry and Boris Prolokov engineered the sting operation to ship arms up the Potomac and store them beneath the Wilson Bridge.

Stone became visibly angrier by the minute as she listened to McCarthy's explanation.

"I can't believe you lied to me!" she yelled finally. "When you prepared that warrant so effortlessly, I should have known something was up. All the time you were writing it, you knew there were no drugs. You just wanted to gather more information for yourself." She was shaking as she added, "You perpetrated a fraud on the courts is what you've done."

McCarthy stared at an empty square of space in the room, as he had done when Stone first shared her theory about drugs being shipped along the river. "At the time I prepared the warrant, I was uncertain whether the facts Morelli was sharing with us comported with the information I'd learned from Landry and Senator Lowenstein," he said, avoiding eye contact.

"That's bullshit!" she spit out. "Don't distort what you did. At least have the courtesy to be truthful now."

McCarthy rose, spreading his arms wide in supplication. "I am being honest. I told you about a confidential meeting I had in the Russell Senate Office Building. And I explained my rationale for deliberately sabotaging a settlement in BOM. I didn't have an obligation to tell you any of those things. I shared them because I believe Landry is involved in something sinister and evil."

"You better come up with something better than that if you want to impress me," Stone scoffed, folding her arms across her chest. "You took advantage of me to secure a warrant to conduct your own private investigation, and I don't like it."

"No. I did it to seek the truth."

Stone stood to leave. "You're a pompous jerk, Mac," she said. "The only truth that exists for you is the one that fits your version of the facts. You twist and you connive. You make me sick."

Lin had sat silently in the room during their exchange. "Listen," she said. Both Stone and McCarthy turned as though they'd forgotten she was there. "I was mad at Mac, too. I've been working alongside him, and I felt betrayed by something he did. But he's leveling now, and that's what matters. We have to work as a team. Otherwise, Landry is going to run circles around us."

"Fuck off, both of you," Stone replied, storming out of the room.

**

Stone sat in her car parked outside the U.S. Attorney's office. Rain pounded on the roof, hood, and trunk. Water swept across the streetlamp in front of her, appearing like snow against the translucent light. The glow from her phone gave her face a bluish cast in the dark cabin of the vehicle as she ran through text messages, phone calls, and emails.

One message jumped off the screen at her. It was from Reese. He had sent it while she was driving on the parkway. It read:

BORIS PROLOKOV WAS ARRAIGNED IN ARLINGTON GEN DIST CT TUESDAY, SEPT 10, REPRESENTED BY SEAN MATTHEWS.

Stone searched for Lin's number and dialed it. "You're right," she said. "We have to work together as a team, or we're screwed. I'm coming back upstairs to share some information with you. I think Boris Prolokov murdered Sean Matthews."

CHAPTER 44

Late in the afternoon, Landry ran to his car in Crystal City, dodging puddles and wrestling with an umbrella turned inside out by the menacing wind.

Anger seethed inside him. The news of Matthews' murder, coupled with that of the missing fisherman, drove him to distraction. As if that wasn't enough, the rain was causing havoc with his planned sting operation.

As soon as he got into his car, the phone rang.

"What is it?" he barked as he slammed the door shut, cutting off the sheet of water cascading down on him.

"Alec Gordievsky bought a ticket to Seattle with a connecting flight to British Columbia," reported one of his subordinates.

"Son of a bitch!" Landry hollered. "I knew he was going to do something like that. Where is he now?"

"He's literally stopped at the light on 23rd Street in Arlington, by the Exxon."

That was only a half mile from Landry's location.

"What kind of a car is he in?" Landry turned on the windshield wipers and cranked up the defroster as he pulled away from the curb and headed along the southbound lane of South Clark Street, which winds through Crystal City like a woodland stream.

"A blue Mazda sedan picked him up," answered the analyst who was tracking the car. "He's in the back seat."

Landry sped through Crystal City. He made a slight right turn and spun the wheel onto the ramp heading toward the airport, pressing the accelerator to the floor and flying up the ramp as though commandeering a rocket. He saw the blue Mazda to his left, executing its own hairpin turn and rising to the point where the ramps intersected. He timed the movement of both vehicles and braced for impact.

He speared the Mazda at breakneck speed, the front driver's side of his car hitting the front passenger side of the other vehicle and ramming it into the Jersey wall. The force of the collision pushed both vehicles 30 feet along the wall.

Landry shoved aside the airbag that had deployed in front of him and worked his way across the front seat to exit the passenger side of his vehicle. In seconds, he was at the rear passenger-side door of the Mazda. He ripped open the door and yanked Gordievsky out of the vehicle.

A Fiat eased past the two cars. It stopped a safe distance ahead near the entrance to the airport. Santana, the car's driver, adjusted his rearview mirror to watch the unfolding scene.

Landry pushed Gordievsky, who was still stunned from the crash, to the ground. He brushed rain and wet hair out of his eyes. "You are not walking away from me," he hollered. "Not now, not when it's all coming down." He punched Gordievsky in the face and stomach, then stood and began kicking him viciously.

Gordievsky took only defensive actions, making no effort to counterpunch.

Both men were now completely drenched. The roadway had turned into a stream, with water racing down the ramps. The befuddled Uber driver stayed in the Mazda. He had dialed 911 and was hollering at the police dispatcher to do something about the madman who had harpooned his car.

A cruiser pulled up alongside the crashed cars. A second later, the cruiser was joined by two large unmarked vehicles. Blue and red lights flashed from the dashboards and rear windows of the unmarked vehicles. Six occupants exited the front and back seats, wearing raincoats and caps. One of them corralled the two police officers who had exited the cruiser. Another went over to the Mazda and spoke to the driver. Others ushered Landry and Gordievsky into one of the unmarked vehicles.

"The ICBM's blasting off," one of them muttered. "It's not going like he planned and it's freaking him out."

Once in the backseat of the vehicle, Landry berated Gordievsky. "Getting rid of Matthews was bad enough, but dumping the body at Jones Point was a disaster," he said. "You and your people are so fucking stupid. And there's a search for a missing fisherman in Maryland. What did you do, kill him too?"

The Russian grimaced, holding his ribs.

"It was the worst possible thing for you people to have done," Landry said. "The bridge will be swarming with cops. Dropping the body at Jones Point was like painting a big red X on the bridge."

Landry was pleased with himself. Gordievsky deserved to be beaten for his insolence. Now the Russian was sure to follow instructions without second guessing anyone, Landry believed.

Gordievsky was wet and cold. He ached from the collision and the beating Landry had given him. His plan to get away had been thwarted. He silently cursed Landry and Prolokov.

CHAPTER 45

Landry's men dropped Gordievsky at the airport. His hair was disheveled, his face cut and bruised, and his clothes were sopping wet. Gordievsky was told to grab another Uber, go back to his place, and wait for further instructions.

The glass doors to the main terminal separated as Gordievsky approached them. He stumbled into the lobby and stopped in front of digital screens updating the schedule of arriving and departing flights. Then he walked down the concourse to a bathroom, where he washed his face, combed his hair, straightened his clothes, and placed cold paper towels under his eyes.

He returned to the concourse and bought a cup of coffee. He drank it while looking through rain-splattered floor-to-ceiling windows at airplanes taxiing across a wet tarmac before lifting off the ground and being swallowed up by the black sky.

Gordievsky considered his options. He was accustomed to life on the sly, mostly fencing stolen goods and shaking down small-time hoods. Currently, he made good money loading crates from the river barge onto trucks on the Wilson Bridge and storing the crates in a warehouse in Anacostia.

But things were turning crazy. A building was incinerated and a man murdered. Gordievsky knew he had abetted the crime; he poured gasoline on the floor of the rickety townhome and he dumped the body at Jones Point. Now he was unable to sleep. He worried about what he had done and the consequences of his actions.

His suspicions about Landry, known to him only as "Phil," were confirmed by the events that unfolded on the airport access road. The local police had arrived in response to an auto collision, but they were turned away by Landry's entourage. "Phil" was not who he claimed to be: Only feds could have persuaded local police officers to retreat, he concluded.

Gordievsky believed Landry was laying a trap for him on the Wilson Bridge. He knew the arms stored at the warehouse were disabled. Either Prolokov was blind or he was conspiring with Landry against the others.

"Fuck this," Gordievsky muttered to himself.

**

Gordievsky awoke early Tuesday morning curled in a fetal position on one of the couches in the airport lobby. He drank the cold remains of the coffee he had purchased the previous evening and returned to the restroom to tidy up. Then he called the Alexandria Police Department.

A minute later, Reese interrupted Stone. "I don't know what it is, but every day I work here I get a weird phone call," he said. "First it was Frank Morelli. Now I have someone on the phone who swears to have information about Sean Matthews' murder."

Stone quickly reached across her desk and put the call on speaker. "Hello," she said. "This is Sherry Stone. I'm the lead investigator in the Sean Matthews murder case. Can I help you?"

"Yes," Gordievsky answered. He had wanted to confess since last night, when the police arrived at the scene of the accident. Instead, he was separated from the police, taken to the airport, and told to get a ride home. "I want to talk to police."

As Stone talked to him, Gordievsky walked past shops and across the walkway leading to the Metro station. An escalator took him down to the baggage area. He exited the airport through the doors to the pick-up area for arriving flights.

Shuttle buses and taxis waited for fares along the curb. People scurried over the crosswalk with luggage on rollers. A cement canopy protected them from the rain. Overhead, other traffic queued to let out passengers for departing flights.

Gordievsky sat on a wooden bench under the canopy. He pulled out a crushed pack of cigarettes, salvaged one, borrowed a book of matches from the smoker seated beside him, and lit the cigarette. All the while, Stone delicately tried to reel him in.

He grew impatient. "I seek asylum," he said. "I am not letting them beat me like a dog. I will talk about murder if you guarantee me protection. I want asylum. And immunity."

Stone replied in a voice she hoped sounded comforting. "I'll help you if I can." She feared she would lose him if she told him the truth, namely that she was not in any position to honor either of his requests. At least she knew where to go for assistance. She could confer with Commonwealth Attorney Katie White about immunity. And Mo Katz must know someone who can help with asylum, she thought. "We need to meet," she said.

"Yes," he replied anxiously. "You need me. I can identify the murderer."

It occurred to Gordievsky that he was at the mercy of a potentially incompetent police officer. Was she as corrupt and dishonest as Landry? If he confided in her, would she help him or feed him to others, and would he be denied any hope of freedom?

Yet putting his trust in this woman was really his only option. And she didn't sound like someone who would kick and punch him on the street, humiliating him. "Okay," he said. "We meet. I know a place."

**

Gordievsky threw his cigarette in a gutter overflowing with water, pulled up his collar, and headed out in the direction of the bike trail that runs along the Potomac River the length of the G.W. Parkway.

Adjacent to the bike trail, airplanes taxied to gates while others lifted off the ground and disappeared in low-hanging clouds. Whirring bursts of engine noise echoed loudly from the perimeter of the airport. Cars, taxis, and buses moved cautiously along the ramp under the G.W. Parkway to the airport in the pouring rain.

Gordievsky quickly disappeared in the storm of perpetual motion, a solitary man unnoticed in a swirl of activity surrounding him. A short distance from the terminal, the bike path forked. Drenching wet, Gordievsky turned left rather than proceed north toward the 14th Street Bridge, and walked through a pedestrian underpass that funneled him into Crystal City. On the other side, he navigated through a small park, went past a concrete wall, and entered a small restaurant camouflaged behind evergreen trees.

Stone and Reese were waiting for him. "We brought you dry clothes," Stone said, smiling. "Hope they fit. Dry off and change, and then we'll talk." Anticipating he would be drenched, Stone had stopped on the way over and bought clothes in a medium size, along with a cheap pair of sneakers. She wished someone had done the same for her yesterday when she drove to the U.S. Attorney's office.

He nodded in gratitude, grabbed the clothes, and headed to the back of the restaurant where the restrooms were located.

He quickly emerged wearing sweatpants and a sweatshirt, both of which were on the snug side. He carried his sodden clothes in one hand, and held the sneakers in the other. "Too small," he said ruefully.

Stone had already ordered breakfast for him and he quickly wolfed it down, without speaking another word. Finally, he wrapped his hands around a hot cup of coffee and started to talk.

The story Gordievsky told was not as helpful as Stone and Reese had hoped. He did not actually witness a murder or even speak to Prolokov about going to Matthews' office. And Prolokov was not there when Gordievsky arrived. Removing the body and dumping it at Jones Point could not be easily traced back to Prolokov, at least not on the basis of Gordievsky's testimony alone.

Plus, Gordievsky did not have clean hands. He torched the townhouse and helped cart Matthews' mutilated body off to Jones Point. In a court of law, he would be viewed as an accomplice after the fact trying to escape punishment by putting the blame elsewhere.

"How can you be sure Prolokov committed the murder?" Reese asked.

"One hundred percent certain," Gordievsky said without hesitation.

Stone believed him. The only question was how to piece together sufficient evidence to charge Prolokov with murder. Scenarios raced through her mind.

"Do you know whether anyone else was with Prolokov and Matthews?" she asked.

"Nyet."

"Would you be willing to wear a wire and help us record a conversation between you and Prolokov discussing the murder?"

Gordievsky spewed a mouthful of coffee onto his plate. "You joke." He wiped his mouth with a paper napkin. "No way. If he finds out, he will kill me." He pointed at Stone and Reese. "You too," he said.

"Then will you come back to the station with us and make a statement?" Stone asked. "We'll protect your identity. If we have enough evidence to arrest Prolokov, and if he confesses to a crime, there will never be any need to pull you into the case.

"In the meantime, I'll talk to people about granting you asylum. I'd be lying to you if I told you I know how it works, or whether we can even do it. But you obviously trust us and you've put yourself at risk by reaching out to us."

Gordievsky appeared tense. Reese wondered if his cooperation was fleeting. "What's your full name?" he asked.

"Alec Gordievsky."

"Any relation to Oleg Gordievsky?" asked Reese.

"No relation, but I have heard of him," said Gordievsky. "He was K.G.B. He came over to your side." Gordievsky seemed to relish the irony. "I will go back with you to station and make statement."

**

Prolokov sat in his car and watched the trio depart the restaurant. The engine, headlights, and windshield wipers were running. Although the windows were slightly foggy, he could identify Gordievsky and the policewoman. He remembered when she looked squarely into the television camera and said, *We will bring this perpetrator to justice.* Ever since that moment, he had wanted to strike out against her.

She fooled him the other night on the parkway. But today he outmaneuvered her and was rewarded for it by stumbling upon her unexpected meeting with Gordievsky. He would deal with all of them in due course.

CHAPTER 46

The second interview with Gordievsky was conducted Tuesday afternoon and yielded no better information. Stone was disappointed, but not surprised. Gordievsky was acting out of anger, not altruism. His direct knowledge tying Prolokov to Matthews' murder amounted to no more than a thin speculative thread that could easily be shredded by an astute defense attorney.

"Are we done?" Gordievsky asked, sensing Stone's frustration.

"Almost," she said, opening a manila folder. She removed a photo and slid it over to Gordievsky. "Do you know this man?"

Gordievsky scowled and nodded. "That is Phil. He is a friend of Prolokov's."

"What can you tell us about him?"

Gordievsky shrugged. "Perhaps it is the other way around," he said. "Perhaps I should be the one asking what you can tell me about Phil." As he asked the question, Gordievsky realized his motivation to contact the police was as much, if not more, to retaliate against Landry than Prolokov.

"You go first," Stone said. "I'll reciprocate. You have my word."

**

After the interview ended, Stone drove to the Commonwealth Attorney's office. She had informed Commonwealth Attorney White about Gordievsky, and White had requested a briefing when the interviews were finished. Dusk descended on the city as Stone drove from the police station to the CA's office. The rain continued unabated.

The outdoor lights of the courthouse ushered Stone into the building. She took the stairs to White's third-floor office. The front office staff had already departed. Seeing the office door open, she stepped inside, knocking on the doorframe as she did so.

"Thanks for dropping by," White said, glancing up and rising from behind her desk. "It's been a long day." She pointed with her hand. "You know Mo."

Katz stood from the chair opposite White. "Is this coincidence?" Stone asked.

"Hardly," White replied. "I asked Mo to join us. I considered it both personal and professional courtesy to keep him informed about our investigation. I didn't think you'd object."

"No objection here," Stone said, giving a nod to Katz.

White suppressed a grin. Everyone knew about Stone's arrest as a rookie cop and how Katz had adroitly maneuvered the case through the court system, getting it dismissed and subsequently expunged. White knew the case better than most; she was the prosecutor Katz had outsmarted.

"Gordievsky claims Prolokov murdered Matthews, but the information he's got is circumstantial," Stone explained. "He didn't see anything or actually talk with Prolokov on the night of the 13th. In addition, his credibility in front of a jury is going to be shit. He's an accessory after the fact. He torched Matthews' office and dumped his body down at Jones Point."

White toyed with a pen as she listened. "That sounds just great," she said. "I wonder what possessed a guy like that to contact the police in the first place?" she asked.

"Curtis saw Landry stomping some young guy in the rain on the airport access road yesterday," Katz interjected. "It must have been Gordievsky. That's probably the act that ignited his rage."

Katz pulled out his phone and texted Santana to join them. Santana, who was in Old Town, texted back he would be there in ten minutes.

As they waited, White pointed to a file folder lying on her desk labeled *Commonwealth v. Boris Prolokov.* "You might want to flip through this," she said to Stone. The file contained information about Prolokov's DWI case. White had retrieved the folder from one of her assistants in preparation for her meeting with Katz.

When Santana arrived, he confirmed that he had witnessed Landry beating Gordievsky on the airport access road.

"Gordievsky told me that he and Prolokov are working with Landry to hide illegal arms under the Wilson Bridge and transport them to a warehouse in Anacostia," Stone said.

Katz nodded in agreement. "Everything the Russian said has been corroborated by the information being assembled by McCarthy and Lin."

"As soon as the rain stops," Stone said, "I'm going out to the bridge. If they're going to try to move the arms, I'm going to stop them."

Santana mentioned Landry being at Belle View Park when the drawbridge was raised. "I drove out onto the bridge after it reopened. I didn't find anything except a cigarette butt."

"It didn't happen to be Sobranie Black Russian, did it?" Stone asked. Prolokov's file rested in her lap. Santana looked at her. "You can tell because it has a distinct golden butt," she added.

"Actually, it was," Santana laughed. "I remember a detail like that. I put the cigarette in the evidence room the day after I retrieved it. I haven't done anything more with it, but I remember thinking at the time it might be significant."

"Super significant," Stone said. "The reason I asked was because we picked up a Black Russian in the alley outside of what remains of Matthews' place."

"That's interesting," said White, putting down her pen and surveying their faces.

"One more thing," Stone said as she tapped the file in her lap. "According to this report, Prolokov never picked up his rental car after it was seized during his arrest. There's a tag in the file, which means the car's still in the impound lot."

"What does that buy us?" asked White.

"Maybe nothing," Stone said, "but if there are Black Russians in the car's ashtray, we could match the DNA to the cigarettes in the alley and on the bridge. It'd be one more data point." She took out her phone and dialed the number on the tag. Stone provided the make, model, and license plate number of the car to the person who answered the phone. "Bingo," she said after a few minutes. Then, looking at Katz, she asked, "Want to take a ride?"

"It can't hurt," he said.

Katz and Stone bade goodnight to White and Santana and headed to her car. Katz was going to say something about Stone's living on Prince Street and Santana cruising through her neighborhood, but decided against it.

As Stone's car emerged from the underground parking lot, rain greeted them. "Shit," Stone said. "It's been raining non-stop since Saturday. When is it ever going to end?"

She turned on the headlights and the rain shimmered in the lights' glow. As Stone drove, Katz told her about his trip to Columbia Bay. He also told her about the robbery of Matthews and Hutton.

Stone, in turn, provided greater detail about the second interview with Alec Gordievsky and his revelations about the goings-on at the Wilson Bridge. "Prolokov murders Matthews while he's assisting Landry in a sting operation," she said. "It doesn't add up."

"I agree," Katz said, "I'd like to figure out what's going on."

"I know just how to do it," Stone said. "As soon as the storm clears, I'm going out to the bridge. They're going to move the crates and I'm going to be there to help them."

Rain fell in torrents. The car's wipers whipped across the windshield, but they hardly helped them see the road ahead. Everything was a blur.

**

The impound lot was pitch black, the only light coming from light bulbs hung from poles sparsely positioned around a perimeter defined by a 10-foot chain-link fence topped with barbed wire.

They got out of the car and ran to the small trailer on the lot. They pushed open the door, bringing water and wind in with them. The rain battered the trailer like a thousand pairs of drumsticks, but the attendant inside did not seem to mind. In response to Stone's request, he took a key off a hook on a large pegboard and handed it to her. He lent Katz a flashlight.

Katz and Stone took the back door that led to the lot and, guided by the light from the flashlight, dodged water-filled potholes to reach the car.

Stone beeped the car key fob. Up ahead, rear lights flashed red. They ran toward the car and quickly jumped in to escape the nonstop rain. Katz flashed his light on the open ashtray in the center of the console. Inside the ashtray were a half dozen cigarette butts glittering in the bright light.

"Sobranie Black Russian," Stone said.

Stone unzipped her raincoat and removed a pair of latex gloves and a plastic bag from an inside pocket. "I'll take these little cancer sticks and inventory them in the property room," she said. "In the morning, I'll notify the lab to pick them up, along with the cigarette I found at Matthews' office. For the time being, I don't need the cigarette that Curtis found at the bridge. Maybe later, but not yet.

"I'm going to interview Prolokov and get a warrant to search his home. Even if he doesn't incriminate himself during the interview, I'm confident we'll find enough evidence to charge him with Sean's murder."

CHAPTER 47

News of the investigation leaked immediately. No one was surprised. There were investigators and lab technicians, the employee at the impound lot, and sundry prosecutors and cops who knew the Russian was a suspect in the Matthews murder case, and it only took one of them to set off a media frenzy. Some even speculated that White or Stone leaked the information to see how Prolokov would react.

By noon Wednesday, Prolokov's home was besieged by reporters and TV crews. They flooded the driveway when a large black SUV pulled up and a tall, lanky middle-aged man in an expensive Italian suit got out and went into the house.

"This is ironic," Jon Bennett said as he greeted Prolokov.

Prolokov shrugged. "I am Russian, so irony is a part of life for me." He invited Bennett inside and introduced him to Jimmy Wolfe, dean of the local bar association, who was standing in the library. "I contacted Mr. Wolfe because I did not hear from you," Prolokov said apologetically. "However, I have not retained him." Turning to Wolfe, he added, "If charges are filed, Mr. Bennett will represent me."

They sat down in the library. Prolokov and Bennett took opposite ends of a long white sofa and Wolfe sat in an ornate lattice chair facing them. A low glass coffee table stood between the sofa and the chair. Two coffee cups and saucers were on the table.

Rain splashed against the windows along the far wall. The windows were framed by heavy, expensive draperies topped with elaborate cornices. A plush Oriental rug covered the hardwood floor where the sofa, chair, and coffee table were arranged.

Wolfe was old, white-haired, and plump, with shrewd, watery eyes and dark eyebrows. He was dressed in a brown blazer and grey trousers, colorful socks, and brown loafers. He picked up one of the cups and finished drinking his coffee.

Bennett laid a pen and legal pad on the coffee table, a sign that no one was to take notes or create a record of their conversation. He leaned back. "Tell me precisely what happened," he said to Prolokov.

"Where do I begin?" asked the Russian.

Bennett folded his long, bony fingers and placed them on his lap. "Tell me what you did after the deed was done."

Wolfe was stunned. Although media reports intimated that strong circumstantial evidence existed against Prolokov, Wolfe would never have begun an interview by asking the client what happened *after the deed was done*. He felt Bennett's inquiry was imprudent and unwise.

Wolfe suddenly felt a sensation on the side of his face. He turned. Bennett's eyes were boring into him.

"Excuse me for a minute," Bennett said, interrupting Prolokov before he had a chance to answer the question. With his eyes trained on Wolfe, Bennett said, "May I speak to you outside for a minute, please?"

They retreated to the foyer. A small antique table with long legs abutted the wall adjacent to the front door. A large mirror in a gilded frame was placed over it. Opposite the mirror a winding wooden bannister and wide stairs led upstairs. Bennett closed the door to the library.

"I saw the look on your face," Bennett said in a bemused tone. "I admit my methods are a bit unorthodox, but I did not ask the client whether he committed a crime. Quite frankly, I don't want to know. If he confesses to the murder, well," Bennett rubbed his hand on his jaw, "well, I'm stuck. I'm precluded from putting him on the stand, you know."

Wolfe nodded. It was one of the cardinal rules of the practice of law: once a client admitted guilt, the attorney could not put him on the stand to deny having committed the crime. The client could remain silent or enter a plea, or claim extenuating circumstances led him to commit the crime, but he could not lie under oath.

"I understand what you're saying," Wolfe said, "but I'm frankly shocked at your approach. You're placing the client at the scene of the crime. However you slice it, you're stuck with whatever story he provides to you. If we walk back into the library and he says the first thing he did was wipe blood off a knife, what are you going to do?"

Bennett put his hand on Wolfe's shoulder. "Don't worry," he said. "I have it under control. Don't question my techniques or I'll have to ask you to leave."

Then he lowered his hand, turned the doorknob, and swung the door open. The men took their seats. Wolfe noticed two crushed cigarettes butts in a saucer that now served as an ashtray. He glanced at Prolokov, who looked nervous.

"So," Bennett said, "let's start again. What did you do?"

Prolokov cleared his throat. "I was standing on a deck in the back of the townhouse," he said. "I recall looking up at the sky and observing the moon, which was extremely bright that night."

"Did anyone see you?" Bennett asked.

Prolokov shook his head. "I don't think so. I remember looking at the parking lot, and wondering if anyone might be there. No one was. I made a phone call and I smoked a cigarette. I might have thrown it on the ground. I don't remember."

Bennett looked at Wolfe. "The cigarette doesn't bother me," he said. "Mr. Prolokov was Sean Matthews' client. He smoked cigarettes outside the law office. It wouldn't be unusual to find a cigarette butt in a parking lot.

"On the other hand, the phone call is problematic. The police will obtain records. Those records will show the client's proximity to the crime." He paused and then added, "But those records might also be an alibi. After all, the body was found at Jones Point. And the fire started at some time after the phone call occurred."

Bennett turned back to Prolokov. "Where did you go after the call?"

"I went to a bar at a hotel in Rosslyn. There will be witnesses. I sat at the bar, drinking."

Bennett nodded approvingly.

CHAPTER 48

While Bennett was questioning Prolokov about events that occurred after the murder, Stone was searching for clues in events that took place prior to the murder. Her inquiry led back to Columbia Bay. To understand what happened there, she called Hutton. "How can I help?" Hutton asked after Stone introduced herself.

"You can begin by explaining why you never testified at the McBride trial," Stone said, recalling Katz's telling her about his trip to Columbia Bay and how it struck him as odd that Hutton got a free pass.

"No one ever contacted me."

"That so?"

"You sound like you don't believe me. Have you heard otherwise?"

Stone was startled by Hutton's defensive posture, which suggested to her that Hutton was withholding information. "Well, I know that attorneys are chummy with one another," she said. It was a bluff, although Stone felt it was not outside the realm of possibility that Hutton had contacted the defense attorney.

Hutton didn't answer. Instead, she asked, "What are you after?" She was already looking for an exit strategy.

"Some honesty," Stone said. "Maybe a little cooperation. After all, you were dating Sean Matthews at the time all of this happened. Don't you have any feelings for him?"

"Listen," Hutton replied bitterly, "I really didn't want to get involved in that case. I told Sean that. He must have communicated it to someone. I'm sorry about what happened to him. I'm a wreck over the whole thing.

"Don't pull at my heartstrings by asking whether I still have feelings for him. It's really none of your damn business. Stick to the facts, Detective Stone, and leave my personal feelings out of it."

Then she added, "Sean left me a phone message shortly before he died. I still have it. I'll find it and call you back."

Satisfied with Hutton's offer, Stone provided her contact information and hung up.

Wednesday night, Landry sat in the conference room staring at the model of the bridge, cradling a ceramic cup filled with hot coffee. Operation Open Sky should have taken place yesterday, the 17th of September. The moment was supposed to be triumphant. Instead, incessant rain had dashed his plans, Sean Matthews was dead and there was speculation that the man missing in Maryland might have been murdered.

Landry felt things spinning out of control. If he could not control the narrative, the entire operation would dissolve. His cohort could be exposed and his methods called into question. Fear and frustration seethed within him. Landry knew others called him "the ICBM" behind his back. He had sought vindication by undertaking a singular audacious act without fully anticipating the risks, until now.

Landry stood up, wound his arm in a pitching motion, and hurled the cup at the model, coffee splashing out as it flew through the air. The ceramic cup struck the model, shattering the drawbridge and scattering the model trucks over the table.

CHAPTER 49

Stone called Prolokov early Thursday morning and asked that he come in for questioning in the Sean Matthews murder case. He arrived at the police station an hour later, accompanied by Bennett. Reese greeted them in the lobby and took them upstairs.

Stone conducted the interview in a small, brightly-lit room about the size of a jail cell, with a small window high up in the far wall. She sat on one side of a table, accompanied by a senior member of the homicide unit. Prolokov and Bennett sat opposite them. Everyone rested their arms, hands, and elbows on the table.

Stone placed a tape recorder in the center of the table. She turned it on, announced the time, 10:10 a.m., and asked the parties to identify themselves. Then she asked Prolokov about his whereabouts Friday night, September 13.

Prolokov looked morose. "I went to visit my attorney, Sean Matthews," he said.

Stone was surprised and slightly apprehensive at this unexpected response. "What time was that?" she asked.

"I don't know. It was late. The moon hung high in the sky. That's all I remember." Prolokov looked around. He studied the cinder block walls, painted light grey. He plunged a hand into the pocket of his jacket and retrieved a book of matches, which he held in his hands. An imprint on the book of matches said "Connexion."

"Do you need to smoke?" asked Stone.

"Not now," Prolokov replied. "But, yes, I smoke, if that's your question. If you found cigarette butts lying outside Sean's office, they are probably mine. I smoked every time I visited him, outside by the dumpster. He was my attorney for a DWI."

Stone smiled wryly. The trip to the impoundment lot with Katz suddenly seemed like a colossal waste of time. Prolokov was showing her that he could wiggle out of whatever traps she might set to catch him.

**

Two black SUVs pulled up to the curb in front of Prolokov's house. Watching from a window, a maid observed occupants jumping from the vehicles and rushing up the walkway. A loud knock followed. She hurried downstairs and opened the door.

Someone handed her a piece of paper and in an instant police stormed through the foyer and into every room, upstairs and downstairs. The maid observed they were all wearing blue gloves. She retreated to a pantry in the back of the residence.

**

"What was the nature of your visit?" Stone asked.

"I knew Sean was back from South Carolina." Prolokov lowered his eyes and studied the book of matches. "I wanted to talk to him."

"About what?"

"About becoming general counsel for my business, Pasha Industries. He was my registered agent in Virginia. I was impressed with the way he was handling my legal matters. I thought he was a good fit."

Stone did not believe a word of what Prolokov said to her. No one with any business sense would hire someone like Matthews as their corporate counsel. Matthews had only accompanied Prolokov to an arraignment on a DWI, hardly a proceeding upon which to judge the attorney's legal acumen, Stone thought to herself.

She pushed back her chair. "I need a minute." She stepped outside and called Reese. "David," she said. "I want you to check records with the State Corporation Commission. Confirm whether Matthews was a registered agent for Pasha Construction, and then check Matthews' bank statements for any retainer from the company." After she hung up, she scanned her phone messages and saw that the search warrant had been executed at Prolokov's home. She returned to the interview room.

"What else did you talk about?" she asked, standing against the wall.

"Nothing. I was only there a couple of minutes."

"What did you do when you left?"

"Actually, I went outside and smoked a cigarette. I called a business associate and asked him to meet me in Rosslyn for drinks."

Prolokov looked at the book of matches. "We met at the Key Bridge Marriott."

"Do you have your phone with you?"

"No."

"What's your friend's name?"

"I don't want to involve any of my friends in this case. In fact, I don't think I want to answer any more of your questions." He turned to Bennett. "If they have a warrant, they can arrest me. Otherwise, I'm ready to go."

Before Bennett could speak, Stone's phone vibrated. She reached over and opened the door again. "I need another minute," she said. She read the text in the hallway outside the room. A serrated knife had been found in Prolokov's home.

**

It was considerably longer before Stone returned this time to the interrogation room. When she did, she served Prolokov with an arrest warrant. As he was taken into custody for the murder of Sean Matthews, a clinician took a sample of his saliva.

Bennett cursed Stone. "It'll never hold," he hollered. "I'll have my client released in a day. And I'll defeat you in court. It'll be easy because you have no evidence."

An hour later, Reese informed Stone that a review of Matthews' online banking account found the attorney had transferred $75,000 from an account in the name of PASHA Industries to his personal account in the early morning hours of Saturday, August 31. The transfer was completed on Wednesday, September 4. Matthews had never spent a penny of it.

**

When he heard the news of Prolokov's arrest, Landry went into an absolute panic. He raced from his office in Crystal City to the Alexandria courthouse. The wipers slapped across the windshield in double time; even so, he barely saw the road ahead.

It was imperative for him to get Prolokov out on bond. Otherwise, he concluded, the entire sting operation would implode. He had already redrawn the plan. As soon as the rain dissipated, the crates would be lifted from the barge to the bridge and transported to the warehouse. The takedown would be executed in less dramatic fashion at the warehouse at the end of the week.

Buried in thought, Landry nearly drove past an empty parking space directly in front of the Alexandria courthouse. He hit the brakes, put the car into reverse, and tucked the vehicle tightly against the curb. Alighting from the car, he jumped over a river of water running along the curb and ran through the rain to the courthouse.

Five minutes later, he was sitting in Commonwealth Attorney White's office. He had no choice but to share information about the sting operation with her. Otherwise, he concluded, it would fail. "He's the linchpin to the entire operation," Landry explained. "You have to release him so that he can get to the bridge. Without Prolokov, the others won't show up."

White expressed incredulity. "For Christ's sake, Phil, the man may have murdered an attorney," she said. "I don't care whether your plan's derailed." She wanted to add that they both knew his contrived terrorist plot was nothing more than a foil to keep the terrorist threat front and center in the public's mind while he advanced his own career. Instead, she bit her tongue and stood her ground.

Landry was taken aback by her intransigence. But rather than pursue a pointless effort with the commonwealth attorney, he retreated. He went back to the elevator and pressed the button for the fourth floor. It was not his preferred option, but he had enough dirt on White's predecessor, Jordin Deale, the city's newest circuit court judge, to push his agenda if he needed to do so.

CHAPTER 50

The bond motion was heard Friday morning at 10 a.m.

"Boris Prolokov," announced the jailer. Prolokov smiled to himself as he was led out of the holding cell into the bright light of the courtroom. Bennett would now work his magic and get him released. A deputy sheriff removed the handcuffs.

Prolokov pulled the cuffs of the starched shirt and squared the shoulders of the charcoal grey suit Bennett had brought him to substitute for the green jumpsuit he had been issued yesterday. He straightened his tie, and, looking at the judge, bowed slightly in deference. Then he sat beside Bennett.

"Mr. Bennett," Judge Deale said, nodding at Prolokov's attorney.

Bennett stood and addressed the court. "There are specific factors for the court to consider in setting a bond in this case," he began. It was a pro forma recitation, one he'd delivered hundreds of times. "These include whether the accused has ties to the community, whether he presents a risk of flight, whether he is a risk to public safety, and whether he has a past record. On all counts, the defendant will demonstrate his fidelity to the court and to the community. I will, therefore, ask the court to set a reasonable bond." He turned his head. "I have witnesses who can vouch for my client's upstanding character."

"Proceed," the judge directed.

Three witnesses testified, including a foreman on one of Pasha's construction projects, a neighbor, and a banker who managed Pasha's business account, each attesting to Prolokov's ties to the community, the unlikelihood of his running, and his peace-loving nature.

When Bennett finished, the judge turned to the prosecutor and asked, "Does the Commonwealth wish to put on any evidence?"

"Yes," said White. "I have two former employees of Pasha Industries with direct knowledge of the type of operation that Mr. Prolokov is operating." Bennett turned slightly to White, then swiveled around as three men entered the courtroom. Prolokov furrowed his brow and leaned over to Bennett, who warded him off. "Not now," Bennett whispered, annoyed.

Bennett rose. "If I may remind the court," he said, "this is not a hearing for disgruntled employees to air grievances against their former employer."

"I'll decide how much weight to assign to their testimony," the judge replied dismissively. She told White to proceed.

White used the witnesses' testimony to paint Prolokov in a harsh light. "He has thugs on the waterfront," one said. "He intimidates the competition, engages in extensive graft, and otherwise runs a corrupt operation, from generating false bills to planting phony stories online about other businesses," said another.

After twenty minutes of blistering testimony, White turned to Bennett. "Your witness," she said.

Bennett evaluated the situation. He had many questions, few answers. What would these two witnesses say on cross-examination, or redirect, to further imperil Prolokov's chances of release? And how would the judge weigh their testimony vis-à-vis the three witnesses who testified for the accused?

Bennett surveyed the room. He looked at the judge, the witnesses, the prosecutor, and his client. "No questions," he said.

"Very good," the judge said. "I'm ready to rule."

"Judge," Bennett jumped up, alarmed by the tone of her voice. "In light of this testimony, I would like a recess of an hour or so, so that I can gather information to rebut the false accusations that have been leveled against my client."

"No," the judge said. "I'm prepared to rule. Both sides offer compelling evidence. Each side describes a different individual. It is impossible for me to ascertain the truth. I must weigh the testimony and assign the credibility I think it deserves." She hesitated, then said: "Bond will be set at $500,000." Pounding the gavel, she rose from the bench and retired behind a large oak door.

Relieved, Bennett sank into his chair. Prolokov grabbed him by the sleeve, excitedly shaking it as a grin spread across his face.

Appearing stunned, White stormed out of the room.

**

Ten percent of the bond was posted in cash, the remainder secured by the equity in Prolokov's residence. At 1 p.m., the Russian retrieved his personal belongings, including his watch and cell phone, and was released from custody. He promised to rendezvous with Bennett in the lobby of the detention center, but managed to find a side exit and depart undetected onto the street. Landry had gotten to him in the lockup and instructed him to act immediately.

Suspecting the phone was monitored or had a tracer installed in it, Prolokov threw it in the trash. He strapped on his Rolex and checked the contents of his wallet. He had neither an umbrella nor a raincoat, but it didn't matter.

After what seemed like forever, the rain relented. Clouds dissipated. A clear sky was forecast by night.

**

Landry pulled out his phone and texted Gordievsky that the crates needed to be hoisted onto trucks and immediately taken to the warehouse. PROCEED WITHOUT DELAY, he wrote, adding that Prolokov had been released from jail and would be joining them. Then he called the bridge operation center.

CHAPTER 51

Stone left her townhome on Prince Street as soon as she heard Prolokov had been released on bond. The street was lined with large oak trees, some of which had lost leaves due to the wind and rain and the cooler autumn temperatures. For the first time in nearly a week, she walked to her car without getting drenched, as the rain was reduced to a light drizzle.

Suddenly, a bullet ripped the edge of her jacket. Stone dove for cover behind parked cars. She cushioned her fall with her hands, which slid across wet mounds of leaves.

Stone had been on edge since being stalked the other night on the G.W. Parkway. Her heightened alertness and quick reactions now saved her life. She crouched and then raced to an eight-foot-high red brick wall abutting the sidewalk and crashed through the low wooden gate, taking cover. The gate swung back, and a second later a bullet splintered one of the gate's slats. It came from directly across the street.

With her back bent against the wall, Stone retrieved her firearm from its holster. She took a deep breath, stood, turned, jumped in front of the waist-high gate, established her stance, and discharged her weapon, five loud blasts in rapid succession. Her target was a man with a gun standing beside a tree behind a parked car. He spun around, fell to his knees, and crumpled on the wet sidewalk.

Stone looked to her left, then her right. Fortunately, no pedestrians had been caught in the crossfire. No cars were coming down the street.

She crossed the street, her firearm held in both hands, and studied the man on the ground, focusing on his close-cropped hair and black leather jacket. She felt for a pulse and was not surprised when there was none. Realizing she might not be the only target, Stone pulled out her cell phone and called Reese. As she did, Santana ran out of the door to her townhouse, both hands on his semi-automatic. He had already called for backup.

**

Reese answered on the third ring. Stone asked him his whereabouts. "I'm on Jefferson around the corner from Faccia Luna,

186

picking up a pizza," he said nonchalantly. "I hope no more rain starts until I make it to the car. Why, where are you?"

"Listen," she said, "someone just tried to kill me. It has to be related to our meeting with Alec Gordievsky. If they're after me, you're probably being followed as well, and your life may be in danger. I want you to stay in the restaurant until I arrive. Do you understand?"

Suddenly Stone heard sounds like firecrackers erupting from the phone, followed by a loud scream. By this time, Santana had reached her side and was staring down at the body. "What happened?" he asked.

"David's been hit!" she screamed. "I've got to get to him."

At that instant, a cruiser arrived, its emergency equipment activated. Red and blue lights flashed up and down the street. Stone jumped into the passenger seat. They were about eight blocks from the restaurant. "Get additional backup to Jefferson and Washington," she instructed the driver. "We have a man down. Go!"

The cruiser raced east at top speed. Its tires squealed as it executed a hairpin turn on Alfred Street. Santana remained on the sidewalk, awaiting additional backup.

**

After firing in Reese's direction, the gunman ran through puddles toward Columbus Street. He heard a siren heading in his direction. He thrust one hand into his pants pocket for the keys to his car while the other hand dropped the gun in the gutter.

Filled with fear and fueled by adrenaline, he ran at super-human speed, confident he could open the door, jam the key into the ignition, push the transmission into drive, and pull away from the sounds closing in on him.

As he opened the door, a cruiser careened around the corner and lurched to a stop beside him. A woman emerged from the vehicle in a burst of uncontrollable rage. She ran toward him. As he tried to close the door, she swung her arm into the car and smashed his face with her fist. He reeled as blows pummeled his face and upper body.

Two more squad cars cornered the car, their emergency equipment flashing red, white, and blue colors on the wet, glassy street.

"That's enough." One of the officers tried to pull Stone away but she shrugged him off and dragged the driver out of the car and tossed him into the middle of the street. Four officers surrounded the car, their weapons drawn. "Don't kill him, Stone. Don't kill him with your bare hands!"

Thirsting for air, Stone lowered her face. "He shot David!" she screamed. "He shot that beautiful kid."

The street flooded with squad cars as additional officers arrived at the scene. Two officers flipped the gunman onto his stomach, pulled his arms back, and slapped handcuffs on his wrists. The man rendered no resistance, his face bloodied and his body sapped of energy. "Don't move," one of the officers instructed as the compliant body went limp on the pavement.

**

As some officers assisted Stone, others converged at Faccia Luna and the area surrounding it. An ambulance raced down the street. The rain had stopped completely. The sun, emerging from behind folds of grey clouds, leaked blinding light across the western sky.

A crowd gathered at the corner of Jefferson and Washington Streets. A doctor had rushed out of her office a half block away and was already administering aid when the ambulance arrived. The victim was a young woman. A man was kneeling beside her, a pizza box on the ground nearby.

**

"Where's Lin?" someone hollered across the acre of cubicles that filled the floor of the U.S. Attorney's office. "Someone find her quick. Something's happened to her fiancé."

"What are you talking about?" someone else hollered back. "She's with her fiancé."

A minute later, someone else ran down the floor to Katz's office to report the unimaginable.

**

Katz jumped into his car and took Duke Street to the Alexandria Hospital. He tried to hold back tears as he drove. The initial reports were that Lin was in critical condition. Katz recalled the first time he encountered Lin and Reese together, when they helped him with the Daingerfield Island murder case. They were young and impressionistic, filled with idealism.

He found jobs for them when he became U.S. Attorney. Now he was rushing to her bedside. He asked himself whether he bore responsibility for tonight's misfortune by putting the young couple in harm's way.

Katz parked his car along the horseshoe-shaped curb in front of the red Emergency sign. He ran inside. Two minutes later, he stepped off the elevator into the surgery unit and Reese's desperate embrace. The front of Reese's Capitals shirt was covered with dried blood. His face was mottled and his bloodshot eyes swam in tear-filled sockets. Just the other night, they were laughing over dinner. Now Lin was fighting for her life.

"It happened so fast," Reese said, burying his face in Katz's shoulder. "Mai came around the corner to greet me. Across the street, someone started shooting. I watched as the bullets ripped through her, lifting her off the ground, and tossing her to the ground like a piece of trash."

Katz held the young law student, whose body rippled with emotion. Reese's hands shook violently as they clutched Katz's neck. A stream of tears flowed down his checks. "If she and the baby die, my life ends too," he said.

Katz tried to convey strength and confidence, as though it was transferable like an electric charge. "She's young and strong," he said. "She'll survive. They'll both survive."

**

Ten minutes later, Katz left the hospital. As he sat in his car, he bowed his head down against the steering wheel and prayed for Lin and her baby. Then he called McCarthy.

"This entire mess is related to Landry's operation on the Wilson Bridge," he said. "We need to put an end to this now."

"Stone's already gone to the bridge to investigate," McCarthy said. "And she's mad as hell."

**

Along stretches of the interstate, large illuminated signs announced to motorists that the Wilson Bridge would be closing in 15 minutes.

CHAPTER 52

A large sign at either end of the Wilson Bridge alerted motorists:
DRAWBRIDGE AHEAD
PREPARE TO STOP
WHEN FLASHING

Lights on the signs were flashing. Metal gates began to lower in front of the drawbridge. Traffic on the bridge ground to a halt in front of the gates.

From Virginia, traffic was backed up a half mile leading onto the bridge. From Maryland, it was bumper-to-bumper traffic for over a mile. Cars that passed by before the gates were lowered dashed safely across the remainder of the bridge and continued their journey, leaving an empty stretch of road behind them.

Dusk loomed. The sky slowly turned from crimson to dark blue. The first star of night sparkled. Lightning crackled across the city's skyline. A bolt exploded directly over the Washington Monument, clearly visible from the bridge.

Stone stood at the entrance of the pedestrian walkway to the Wilson Bridge. She wore sneakers, black tights, and a baggy sweatshirt that hid her service revolver. She tried to clear her head of the fear, anger, and frustration caused by the shootings.

A cool breeze swept over the river and the bridge, rushing down the walkway and brushing against Stone. She texted a short message to Santana. She finished listening to the song streaming on her phone. It was "Heroes" by David Bowie and Brian Eno. She removed her earplugs, turned off the music, and tucked the phone in her sweatshirt's pouch. Then she headed onto the bridge, vengeance in her eyes.

**

People materialized at the door to McCarthy's office, including prosecutors, investigators, and military personnel on detail. They coalesced around him eager to acquire information, offer assistance, and prepare next steps. Something was happening; they wanted to be part of it.

McCarthy explained what was going on. "Illegal arms are being stored under the Wilson Bridge," he announced. "The drawbridge has been used like a trapdoor in the floor of a stage to pull those arms up from a barge and onto trucks for transport to a warehouse in Anacostia. It's part of an operation staged by Phil Landry to capture some self-proclaimed terrorists."

He looked at their shocked and surprised faces. "Landry tried to blackmail a judge into releasing one of the terrorists earlier today. The whole operation may be going sideways and might be spilling over into the streets of Alexandria, resulting in the shots that were fired a short time ago."

The crowd grew larger, with fellow prosecutors and others filling the small office. McCarthy's seemingly abysmal performance in the BOM settlement was forgotten and forgiven, with some of his co-workers nodding in admiration as they realized there had always been a method to his madness.

McCarthy grabbed his phone and punched in some numbers. Landry answered the call. He wasn't expecting McCarthy to be on the other end. "What do you want?" he asked, annoyed.

"Mai Lin was shot an hour after Boris Prolokov's release from jail," McCarthy said. "Whatever kind of scam you're running on the Wilson Bridge, you need to end it now. You're putting innocent lives at risk. It's time to launch your takedown operation and arrest those thugs."

Santana walked into the room and flashed his mobile phone. "It's Stone," he said. "She just texted she's on the bridge."

"Did you hear me, Phil?" McCarthy said loudly into the phone. "We have a police officer on the bridge." He choked back tears. "And one of our research assistants is in the hospital fighting for her life. It's time to act!"

Landry sat immobilized. *Mac McCarthy was not going to tell him when to launch Operation Open Sky.* He was about to tell McCarthy to go to hell when two of his lieutenants entered his office. They had heard about the shootings of an Alexandria police officer and a pregnant legal research assistant. By the looks on their faces, Landry knew he was going to be overruled.

"It's all systems go, Phil," one of them said.

CHAPTER 53

Stone jogged along the walkway as the gates dropped. She passed a stenciled marker on a jersey wall that read WWB MILE 0.6. She was now six-tenths of a mile out on the bridge, but still over land. To her left, a railing overlooked white tombstones at a cemetery below; to her right, a high concrete wall separated the walkway from lanes of traffic.

She continued jogging past the marker that read WWB MILE 0.7.

The walkway coursed upward. Stone glanced to her left. The cemetery was now replaced by tiny patches of barren community gardens and gabled roofs of townhouses. To the right, the concrete barrier was gone, replaced by huge sheets of Plexiglas. She could see the lanes devoid of the usual traffic.

A short distance ahead, a man held out his arms, his palms facing her. He was shouting something at her. As she jogged a little closer, she could hear him. "You have to turn back," he hollered. "The drawbridge is opening. You can't continue across the bridge."

A determined look crossed her face as Stone kept jogging steadily toward the man. She passed the marker reading WWB MILE 0.8. Off to her left, Jones Point was visible below, its embankment hugging the river where Matthews' body had been found a week earlier.

"Didn't you hear me?" the man hollered, waving his arms. "You have to turn back."

She sped up. When she reached him, she turned, whipping a leg in the air and catching the man's chin with her sneaker. Her entire body lunged through the air. He fell backwards, hitting the pavement hard. She struck him twice in the torso, flipped him around, pulled his hands behind his back, and quickly slapped a handcuff on his wrist. She spun the other handcuff around the metal railing along the jersey wall.

"What the hell!" he wailed.

She pulled a pair of gloves from her pocket and stuck them in his mouth. "Shut the fuck up, asshole." Then she pulled off his belt, looped it around one of his legs, and tied the other end to the railing.

"This ought to hold you long enough," she said, admiring her handiwork before continuing along the walkway.

She was now at a marker reading WWB MILE 0.9 and standing over water. To the left, upriver, landing lights flickered at Reagan National Airport. Further, the Washington Monument and dome of the U.S. Capitol were visible along the D.C. skyline. To the right, only a jersey wall and a metal railing separated the walkway from the highway.

Suddenly a loud sound screeched over the bridge like a metal monster awakening as night fell on the river.

Stone jumped over the jersey wall and onto the empty traffic lanes on the far side of the gates. She looked down and realized she was standing near the metal lip of the drawbridge. That section of the bridge shook and jerked and slowly began to rise.

She raced forward and catapulted over the lip of the drawbridge like Evel Knievel clearing a ramp at Caesars Palace on his Triumph Bonneville t120 motorcycle. She hoped to make it across, expecting both sides of the drawbridge to be rising and separating in tandem, like a pair of scissors. To her surprise, only the Virginia side of the drawbridge rose. Stone tumbled through space and landed on the level surface of the other half.

Below, billowing in the wind and strapped to the side of the bridge was the huge tarp with the word PASHA emblazoned on it. A speedboat languished in the water adjacent to the tarp. Behind the large flapping canvas, a wooden platform floated on the water. Propelled by a small engine, the platform maneuvered toward the drawbridge.

The side of the drawbridge that rose shuddered to a stop as it formed a 90 degree angle to the bridge, serving as a metal screen blocking the sightline of motorists stopped on the Virginia side of the bridge. Drivers stopped on the Maryland side were at a distance from where the drawbridge rose and could see only a vague shimmer ahead where the metal met the sky.

There was now an empty space in the bridge. A large SUV was parked at the edge of the hole, which looked down to the water below. A string of four flatbed trucks idled in the far lane. A crane was positioned in the center of the bridge adjacent to the hole.

The passenger door of an SUV parked beside the nearest flatbed truck opened and a man got out. As he walked toward the crane, he drew a half-smoked cigarette from his lips and threw it into the air. The cigarette fell into the hole and dropped to the water below.

The operation to retrieve the crates was underway. Hanging over the open span of the bridge, the crane exerted its mechanical muscles as its tightly-wound steel coil spun like the spool on a fishing rod. Slowly, a heavy box was lifted up from the floating barge.

Three men stood at the edge of the open span. They were all tall and swarthy, with close-cropped hair the color of coal. Six others milled about on the bridge. And two others sat in the cabins of flatbed tractor trailers.

A noise suddenly filled the air, a pulsating sound caused by a blade hitting the wake vortex of the previous blade, a phenomenon known as "blade slapping."

Stone knelt beside a jersey wall on a lane opposite the SUV, flatbed trucks, and crane. She looked up, as did the men on the bridge, trying to identify the source of the sound. To the west, lights cut through the clouds, drawing closer by the second.

The crane dropped a large wooden crate onto the bridge. The workers quickly split it open. One of the men removed a sidewinder missile launcher. He hoisted the weapon onto his shoulder and pointed it in the direction of the sound, which he and the others now realized were three rapidly approaching helicopters.

"Oh, my god," Stone said aloud. The whir intensified as the choppers drew closer, the silhouette of their rotating blades and dark bodies clear against the last light of day.

**

An SUV carrying Katz tore across the Eisenhower Valley. It jumped the curb onto northbound Route 1 and turned down the ramp for traffic exiting the bridge on the Virginia side of the river. The SUV raced along the empty lanes that normally would carry traffic from Maryland to Virginia. The vehicle stopped abruptly when it reached the open span.

The helicopters were now positioned above the open bridgespan.

**

Stone popped up from behind the Jersey wall and fired her service revolver at the man balancing the sidewinder on his shoulder. She hit him in the leg. He stumbled. The others turned, drew their firearms, and returned fire. She ducked back behind the wall.

The man holding the Sidewinder hobbled into the middle of the road, pointed the weapon upward, and fired.

The bridge trembled as a streak of light blasted into the air, a plume of smoke and fumes behind it. The small missile struck one of the helicopters, spewing its innards across the sky. The helicopter's twirling blades stopped rotating. It fell straight down like a bird struck by a hunter and crumpled as it hit the pavement of the two HOV lanes, causing a horrific crash that shook the bridge.

The other two helicopters broke formation. One peeled off to the left at 45 degrees, heading toward Jones Point. The other helicopter maneuvered just as quickly to the right, banking toward the Ferris wheel at National Harbor.

Suddenly, on the Maryland side of the bridge, the sound of police sirens and emergency equipment pierced the air. The darkening sky erupted into an array of red, blue, and white emergency lights. An assemblage of police cruisers, vans, fire trucks, ambulances, and SUVs that had driven up the exit lanes stormed across the three empty lanes of traffic and raced at breakneck speed toward the enemy forces gathered around the crane.

Simultaneously, two Coast Guard cutters zoomed south from Haines Point on the D.C. side of the river. A third launched from Jones Point. All three were converging on the bridge.

The men on the bridge turned their attention from Stone and began firing their semiautomatic weapons at the approaching army of police vehicles. Billowing clouds of smoke from the helicopter lying in the HOV lanes wafted across the bridge and created a barrier between the men and the onslaught of vehicles headed in their direction.

In the chaos, one of the men broke ranks, ran to the edge of the bridge, and dove off into the blackness below.

The battery of law enforcement vehicles burst through the cloud of smoke like Patton's tanks at Meuse-Argonne. The vehicles stopped and executed 90 degree turns, forming a shield that faced the men standing around the crate. Officers jumped out of the vehicles and began firing. Their arsenal of weapons dwarfed the firepower of their adversaries, who were caught off-guard and unable to retrieve the weapons in the crates to make use of them.

Warring factions exchanged gunfire. Bullets struck the bridge at awkward angles, their sounds echoing across the bridge and over the water, the sound of metal against metal, now a firestorm created as the two sides confronted one another. The men unloading the crates scattered, some seeking shelter from a mounting barrage of bullets by ducking behind the metal container lifted from the barge while others sought refuge inside the crane.

The helicopter that had veered toward the Virginia shoreline now turned back to the bridge and landed, dumping a handful of heavily armed warriors into the middle of the firefight. The occupants of the vessel from Jones Point had scaled the bridge and were now dropping over the Jersey wall and joining ranks with the others. The cascade of vehicles from Maryland screeched to a halt as law enforcement officers jumped out as an additional offensive line.

Another one of the terrorists ran the length of the bridge, hoping to jump off of it. A frightening barrage of bullets shredded his clothes and sliced his body into myriad pieces, pulverizing him into mist.

A small group on the barge fired blindly up at the opening at the top of the bridge.

Law enforcement directed its fire down the hole, blasting everything in sight. Flesh ripped, wood splintered, metal punctured, water bubbled, bone cracked and blood spurted.

Outgunned and outnumbered, with their numbers rapidly dwindling, the remaining terrorists tossed down their arms and stepped out from behind their makeshift protective barriers with their hands raised.

Two additional helicopters appeared and landed on the Virginia side of the half-raised drawbridge, picked up Katz and others, and safely deposited them on the other side of the bridge with the smoldering carnage.

**

Stone was on her hands and knees on the bridge, her body covered in grit. Katz ran up beside her. They embraced. Despite wearing body armor beneath her loose-fitting running clothes, Stone did not escape injury completely; her left arm was grazed by a stray bullet.

Fires burned on the bridge. Glass and metal were strewn everywhere. The smell of flesh and blood saturated the air. The hulk of the helicopter lay in the HOV lanes, its silver blades twisted like ribbons.

Stone looked at Katz. "Right on time," she said wanly.

"Like I said the other day, they mint badges for people like you," he said. Then, turning, he screamed at the top of his lungs, "Get an ambulance over here right away."

Restless winds blew across the bridge. Santana arrived and embraced Stone. "You did great," he said. "Fearlessly great."

**

After the commotion died down, people stranded on the bridge ventured out of their vehicles and stood speechless. Those who hadn't cowered in their cars during the battle had captured every second of it on their mobile phones. The images went viral, appearing on devices around the world in an instant.

"That was unbelievable," someone texted from the edge of the bridge. "Incredible," texted another. The superlatives suddenly sprang from a thousand mobile devices held by stunned and sober witnesses on the Maryland and Virginia sides of the river. "Audacious." "Ridiculous." "Awesome." "Unreal." "Fucking unbelievable."

CHAPTER 54

Prolokov survived a 70-foot vertical leap from the bridge. When he hit the water, he discarded the shoes, tie, and jacket that he had worn in court. He swam to the platform beneath the bridge, untethered the aluminum fisherman's boat, jumped into it, and drifted beneath the bridge to the Maryland shore. With everyone focused on the firefight, his movements were undetected. Shivering and drenching wet, he crept through shadows to the parking garage of the MGM Grand Hotel.

Everyone in the complex was on the terraces watching the aftermath of the firefight on the bridge. Prolokov found an unoccupied car with the engine running. He drove it onto I-295 and then into D.C. by the old RFK Stadium.

He stopped near the Congressional Cemetery. Dazed, cold, and wet, he sat in the front seat for an hour with the heater turned on full blast to dry his clothes and warm his body.

Eventually, he left the vehicle and wandered toward Barney Circle. Despite his disheveled appearance, he persuaded a dog walker to lend him a phone. He dialed a number. "I'm in Southeast," he said. "I don't know what the hell just happened." He looked at a street sign. "I'm somewhere on Pennsylvania Avenue."

The response was calm. "Cross M Street. You'll see the Anacostia Riverwalk Trail. Walk down to the river. Turn left and take it upriver toward the boathouse at Evans Point. I will meet you there in fifteen minutes."

**

Two hours later, Katz was home, sitting on the porch of his townhome. He had showered, eaten, and changed into shorts and a light pullover sweater. He sat in a wicker chair, sipping a Port City lager and reviewing hundreds of emails and text messages on his phone.

The battle on the bridge broke just before the nightly news. All of the networks led with the story. Katz was filmed racing to Stone's side. Afterwards, he was interviewed by the local NBC affiliate and by CNN. His phone was deluged with messages from friends, co-workers, and the courthouse crowd.

An hour later, breaking news announced the successful raid at the warehouse and the recovery of the arms stored at that location.

Before he responded to a plethora of messages, including ones from Hutton, Senator Lowenstein, and Snowe, he called the hospital. Reese picked up on the first ring and gave him the good news.

"They're both going to make it," he said excitedly. "She's okay, Mr. Katz, and so is the baby. She's still in intensive care, but they're going to live." He started to sniffle, then cry. "She's so strong, Mr. Katz. She held on for all of us. I am so blessed." Then he started bawling.

Katz's eyes welled. "Thank God, David. That's great news. You're all blessed."

"What a show you put on tonight, Mr. Katz," Reese said, laughing, wiping away tears. "I watched it on the news. It's the only thing they're showing. Is everyone okay? How is Detective Stone?"

"She's fine," Katz said. "She launched that attack singlehandedly. Even if the cavalry hadn't arrived, I think she would have won the battle all by herself. Most amazing law enforcement officer I ever met."

After they finished, Katz called Hutton. She was ready to settle BOM. The timing seemed right. She accepted the terms he had laid out at their previous meeting.

Next, he called the senator. Lowenstein apologized for trusting Landry too much and sharing too little information. "I'll never admit it in public," he said, "but I'm complicit in tonight's insanity." Four law enforcement personnel were dead, including the two-man helicopter crew killed in the crash and two officers who sustained fatal injuries during the firefight. "I'm just glad it wasn't worse than it was," said the senator.

The longest conversation was with Snowe. He broke down as he talked about the brutal attack on Lin, Stone's relentless courage, and the horror he witnessed on the bridge. "It was like being in a war zone," he explained. "All kinds of crazy thoughts run through your mind. Fortunately, none of them came to pass and we prevailed."

"I'm so glad you're okay," she said. "I was worried, and scared." Then she added, "We need to talk about the future. Life is too precious. I don't want to go through it without you." She added that she was returning home as soon as her mom got out of intensive care.

"Okay," Katz said uneasily. "I don't want to go through life without you, either."

He spent the next hour reading tweets, texts, and emails and streaming YouTube clips posted from the scene by onlookers. He slumped over in the wicker chair as fatigue claimed his body and mind.

CHAPTER 55

The Wilson Bridge remained closed until noon Saturday. It took half the night to lower the drawbridge, remove the dead and wounded, clean the debris from the helicopter, and clear the cars stranded on the bridge. Trucks, buses, and other commercial traffic took alternative routes while the bridge was closed.

Beginning in the early morning, throngs assembled along the pedestrian walkway, many of them carrying American flags that they draped over the railings.

Sensing an opportunity to capitalize on the uptick in patriotism precipitated by the incident, politicians sprang into action. By early afternoon, a stage was cobbled together at Jones Point, with the bridge as backdrop, and decorated with patriotic bunting. White folding chairs were arranged in a semicircle around the stage. Local, state, and national politicians rushed to the scene in motorcades to express their support for the swift action taken to stifle the terrorist plot.

Senator Lowenstein's press secretary revised the senator's 9/11 speech, which was uploaded onto teleprompters positioned on either side of the stage. The senator stood at a podium in the center of the stage, flashing a V sign for victory. The celebratory atmosphere was infectious, with lots of cheering and clapping. People were recognized for extraordinary valor, including Stone, whose left arm was in a sling from the bullet that had grazed her.

At Katz's insistence, seats were reserved for Frank Morelli and Jane Hutton. Morelli said he would have felt slighted if he had not been invited, but Hutton expressed surprise. After all, she admitted, she had deliberately tried to take advantage of McCarthy in the BOM negotiations.

"There's no reason for you to include me in this celebration," she said in mild protest when she and Katz encountered one another.

"I beg to differ," he retorted. "You fought hard for your client, but you didn't fight dirty. In the end, you negotiated an end to the case. We're announcing the settlement today. You belong here."

Over Katz's objections, Senator Lowenstein insisted that Landry be recognized for his contributions. The head of the antiterrorism unit basked in the limelight, telling the media how he staged a series of illegal arms transactions as a prelude to Operation Open Sky.

Neither Landry nor Katz had a good word to say to one another when they crossed paths on Jones Point.

"You forced my hand yesterday," Landry said. "My preference was to transfer the arms to the warehouse and to execute the takedown later in Anacostia. Fortunately, it turned out better than I could have hoped." He looked around, contentedly. "I missed my target date, but that was about it."

"Unfortunately, your man Prolokov got away," Katz said pointedly.

"He wasn't 'my man.' Prolokov is the head of a terrorist cell. He's missing, from what I understand. But we'll catch him. There's a manhunt underway now."

"But he was your inside man in putting together this operation, wasn't he?"

"Go back to school, Mo," Landry scowled. "That's the dumbest thing I've ever heard you say, and I've heard some pretty stupid comments come out of your mouth." Landry pressed close to Katz. "Don't waste your time looking into how I put together Operation Open Sky. It's a huge success. Leave it be."

"How about the fact you tried to blackmail Judge Deale into releasing Prolokov on bail?" Katz asked, undeterred.

"We all have our version of the events," Landry responded. "My recollection is I wanted to get Prolokov out on the bridge for the takedown, and she obliged. You'll be hard-pressed to come up with a more compelling storyline, but go right ahead and try, if you like."

"I'm not trying to discredit you, Phil," Katz said. "I just want the truth."

Landry jabbed his forefinger into Katz's chest. "You're not interested in truth, Mo. Save your antics for some naïve sap. Stay out of my business if you know what's good for you."

Katz stepped back, surprised by Landry's attitude. He always expected Landry to be audacious, but this was different. Landry was exhibiting fear, not arrogance. And Katz, detecting it, wondered what Landry was hiding.

Several dozen seats were also reserved for a very special contingency, the families of the BOM victims. When it came Katz's turn to take to the podium, he turned to them and announced the settlement. "Three weeks ago, you visited my office and requested that we seek criminal as well as civil penalties," he said. "I'm honored to tell you today that we succeeded on both counts. I'm grateful to Mac McCarthy, Mai Lin, and a dedicated team at the U.S. Attorney's office. Mostly, however, I'm indebted to you. Your courage and resolve were instrumental to pushing us to do the right thing. We did it for your sons and daughters, for your husbands and wives, and loved ones, whose lives were lost due to the misdeeds of the merchants of death."

When the ceremony ended, Richard Bellows approached Katz. He was holding hands with a woman and a young child. "This is my sister-in-law, Cindy, and my niece, Molly," he said. "They flew in early this morning after hearing the news about the attack on the bridge."

Katz lifted the little girl in his arms. As he did so, a flyover roared across the sky. Their thunderous sound reverberated along the river and through Jones Point Park.

"I want to become president when I grow up," Molly said, looking up. "I want a world where people like my daddy don't die to keep people free. I want everyone to be happy and to love one another."

"Pretty special little girl," Katz said as he handed Molly to her mother. "I'm glad you were able to make it. I know it means a lot to your in-laws."

Jets thundered across the sky. Molly pointed her finger up to the heavens. The crowd cheered until their voices were hoarse.

**

Katz departed in an ebullient mood. As he walked back home, a mile away, his phone vibrated. He removed it from his pocket. A text message from Stone read:

Prolokov found dead in car on M Street SE.

CHAPTER 56

Katz immediately phoned her. "What details can you share?" he asked.

"The Russian's throat was slit with a serrated blade," Stone said. "The butcher's work was identical to Matthews' killing." She let him digest the information, and then added: "It's brazen, Mo. Whoever did this wants us to know he was involved in both murders. He's laughing at us."

Katz walked through a residential neighborhood filled with tidy brick townhomes, meditating on the unexpected turn of events. He came to an intersection with a Don't Walk sign instructing him to stop. Thoughts flashed through his mind. The weapon used to murder Matthews had been recovered in Prolokov's home. The case seemed like a slam dunk. Now, suddenly and unexpectedly, there was another murderer afoot.

"I'm stunned," he said.

"Events haven't exactly gone as we anticipated, have they?"

"That's an understatement," he replied, recalling the series of events that occurred in rapid-fire succession the previous day.

After failing to convince Commonwealth Attorney White to release Prolokov, Landry had visited Judge Deale. He threatened to expose her for an old allegation of sexual harassment unless she released Prolokov. The judge acquiesced, and then immediately reported the incident to the police. The police contacted White, who in turn reached out to Stone and Katz.

They decided to pull their own sting operation on Landry by allowing Prolokov to be released on bond. The assumption was that the Russian would meet up with Landry, at which time both would be arrested. Instead, an unimaginable sequence of events unfolded, beginning with the events on the Wilson Bridge and culminating with Prolokov's murder.

The sign turned to Walk and Katz crossed the street. "Any leads?" he asked.

"Steve McBride," Stone said.

Her utterance caught Katz off guard. "McBride?" he asked, incredulous. He remembered mentioning McBride's name to her the night they drove to the impoundment lot, but he never suspected McBride of being involved in Prolokov's murder. "What makes you bring up his name?"

"A hunch," she said. "Actually, a little more than a hunch."

Katz wondered what information Stone had dug up on McBride. He stopped and sat on a wooden bench outside Misha's coffee shop on King Street. Someone came out of the store, handed him a latte, and mouthed "Thank you." Feeling uncomfortable discussing scenarios while seated on a public sidewalk, Katz said, "Listen, I'm going to grab an Uber and join you at the station in about fifteen minutes."

While she waited, Stone called Gahagan in Columbia Bay. After accepting congratulations for the events of the past day, Stone got down to business. "I'm curious to know whether you still have the contents of Sean Matthews' wallet from the robbery," she said to the prosecutor.

"We had photocopies of the cash and an inventory of the contents of his wallet," Gahagan replied. "Defense counsel stipulated to all of it during trial. After the acquittal, he moved to seal the file. Those exhibits may be packed up by now, along with all the paperwork in the case. I'll check on it on Monday."

Stone thanked Gahagan. Next she called Joey Cook, the custodian of the property room in the Alexandria Police Department. She knew Matthews' wallet was found on his body at Jones Point and taken to the property room for safekeeping. She asked Cook to retrieve the wallet and an inventory of its contents, and then get back to her.

Then she sent an email to one of her investigators to run a forensic search on McBride and his credit cards, phone records, and E-Z Pass, and to search any closed-circuit TV footage available at airports to find out McBride's whereabouts on the weekend Matthews was killed.

When Katz arrived, Stone told him about her calls to Gahagan and Cook.

"What are you thinking?" he asked.

"I'm thinking McBride didn't rob Matthews for money," she said. "He robbed Matthews for some other reason. I think he was after something in Matthews' wallet."

She moved around the room as she spoke.

"As I understand the facts as you explained them to me the other night, McBride collided with a pedestrian after the robbery took place. Assuming McBride was after something in the wallet, the collision might have occurred before he had a chance to remove it. In that scenario, the item remained in the wallet, which was returned to Matthews after the robbery.

"If I'm right, McBride never got what he was seeking. It's possible that the item – whatever it was – was so important to McBride that he followed Matthews to Virginia, murdered him, and then removed it from the wallet."

Katz cocked his head to the side.

"It's a long shot, I know," Stone said. "But I can actually prove my theory, which is why I called Gahagan and Cook. If I'm right, and something was taken from the wallet after the murder, then the contents of the wallet in Columbia Bay will include one or more items than the contents recovered from the wallet at Jones Point. If that's the case, we have a motive for murder."

Stone glanced at her phone. An orange light on the console alerted her of a missed call. She walked around to her computer, stroked a letter on the keyboard, and pulled up the missed call on her Outlook. It was a message from Jane Hutton that included the recording from Matthews that Hutton promised to send to Stone. Stone played the message for Katz.

"Jane, Sean. Listen, I'm sorry to bother you. And I know I've been a real shit. But that's not why I'm calling. I need to tell you something. I met with Steve McBride to apologize for falsely identifying him. As we parted, he said, 'By the way, Sean, did you buy any formal clothes at Columbia Bay or did the casual attire suffice?' Or something like that. That's what we were discussing in the restaurant that night. It's the only place he could have heard it. Can you believe it? He was the one who robbed me, who robbed us. I just thought you'd want to know."

As they listened, Stone looked at her desk. Photos of Prolokov's body faxed by the D.C. homicide unit were on top of a mound of paperwork. She picked up one of the photos. "Suppose McBride and Prolokov knew one another," she said after she turned off the recording.

"*That's* a long shot," Katz said.

"Maybe not," she said. "We downloaded calls from Prolokov's phone that were made to a number in Columbia Bay around the time Matthews went there with Hutton. We're tracing the number now."

Stone paced the room excitedly, waving the photo. "Don't you see how it could all tie together? Prolokov may have inadvertently given Matthews something when they first met in Matthews' office. It might have been a business card or a slip of paper, small enough to slip into the wallet. And maybe it contained information about the arms shipment, something that Prolokov could not afford to become public.

"We know from our investigation that the illegal arms were being stored at Prolokov's construction site around the same time he visited Matthews. We also know that Matthews went to Columbia Bay a couple of days after Prolokov retained him."

Stone tapped the photo against the edge of the desk. "If Prolokov knew Matthews was going to Columbia Bay, he could have contacted McBride to intercede on his behalf. Maybe McBride followed Matthews to the restaurant, where he staged the robbery. Maybe Prolokov and McBride went to Matthews' law office together on the 13th and murdered him."

"Maybe, maybe not," Katz said, skeptically.

"I'll know as soon as I hear back from Gahagan and Cook," Stone said. She dropped the photo back on her desk and returned to the computer. "I'm emailing you a copy of Matthews' message to Hutton," she said, striking the keyboard. "Sean's telling us it's McBride."

CHAPTER 57

Early Monday morning, Gahagan contacted the Clerk of the Circuit Court in Columbia Bay. She learned the evidence admitted at trial had not yet been placed under seal. As a result, she went to the clerk's office, made copies of the contents of the wallet, and forwarded the information electronically to Stone and Katz, along with a copy of the incident report and Matthews' statement.

A list of the contents of the wallet included the following items:

A Virginia State Bar card.

A medical insurance card.

A gasoline credit card.

A Starbucks card.

Two debit cards, one from a bank and the other from a credit union.

A VISA credit card.

A Metrocard.

A voter identification card.

A card from CVS.

An Alexandria City Library card.

A business card belonging to Boris Prolokov.

Upon receipt, Stone compared the list to the contents of the wallet recovered at Jones Point, which had been provided earlier in the morning by Cook. "There's one fewer item on Cook's list," she said triumphantly to Katz. "There's no business card."

Stone printed the card that Gahagan had sent to them. On the front card was the name "Boris Prolokov, President, Pasha Construction Co." On the back were scribbled the words Gadfly, Igla, Strela, and Mistral.

Those words meant nothing to her. She went online and performed a word search. At first, Gadfly seemed harmless. Wikipedia had the following definition:

A gadfly is a person who interferes with the status quo of a society or community by posing novel, potentially upsetting questions, usually directed at authorities. The term is originally associated with the ancient Greek philosopher Socrates, in his defense when on trial for his life.

But Stone found another, far more menacing, definition. Gadfly was a name associated with the same kind of surface-to-air missile system alleged to have taken down Malaysia Airlines Flight 17. The other names – Igla, Strela, and Mistral – were of Russian and French shoulder-fired systems or MANPADs.

"These were the types of systems shipped up the Potomac as part of Landry's sting operation," Stone said.

Her fingers continued to hit the keyboard and pull up articles about the missiles.

"Listen to this," she said, scrolling down to a 2006 Report to Congress by the Congressional Research Service. She read, "Shoulder-fired surface-to-air-missiles have been used in conflicts such as the Arab-Israeli Wars, Vietnam, and the Iran-Iraq War. Afghan mujahideen may have downed 269 Soviet aircraft using shoulder-fired SAMs during the Soviet-Afghan War, and 12 Allied aircraft were shot down during the 1991 Gulf War by MANPADS."

She looked up from the screen. Light from the monitor reflected in her eyes. "Don't you get it?" she asked. "Prolokov wrote the names of arms systems on his business card and inadvertently gave the card to Matthews. The robbery and the murder were pieces of the same crime to prevent any public disclosure about the existence of the MANPADS. If Matthews or someone else pieced together the information on the card, they could have exposed the entire operation. Prolokov could not afford to let that happen."

**

By Monday night, Stone had uncovered additional information. Records from Prolokov's phone showed he had called Columbia Bay around the time Matthews was there with Hutton. Prolokov also received a call from an unknown party on Tuesday, September 3rd, the night of the robbery. Stone surmised both communications were with McBride. According to incomplete phone records and credit card information, she also concluded McBride could have been in D.C. for a one-week period beginning on Friday the 13th.

She reached Katz at his office. "We have our man," she said. "McBride had the time, opportunity, and motive to commit both murders."

Katz hesitated before speaking. He had been listening over and over to Matthews' message to Hutton. It was still rattling around in his brain.

"What's the matter?" Stone asked.

"I'm trying to recall where else I learned about the conversation between Matthews and Hutton," he answered. "I either heard or read it somewhere, but I'll be damned if I can remember where or when."

"I don't see where that's going to get you. I've got our man. Do you have a problem?"

He did. "You've been making assumptions with sketchy facts," Katz said, reluctantly. Stone was a good cop and he did not want to second-guess her. "You know as well as anyone that the only thing worse than an unsolved crime is leveling a charge against an innocent party. I'm worried that you're trying too hard to solve the murders. You need to move more cautiously."

"I'll keep that in mind," Stone replied dismissively. She expected accolades from Katz and was disappointed when she did not receive his praise. She hung up the phone.

**

Stone sat at her desk assessing the case. She felt there were sufficient facts to justify a search of McBride's residence and she intended to share her conclusion with Gahagan. Stone now believed Prolokov and McBride acted in concert to murder Matthews and that McBride subsequently murdered Prolokov to ensure his silence.

Discarding Katz's trepidation, Stone dialed Gahagan. She shared the information in her possession and said she could fly down to Columbia Bay in the morning. "Come on down," Gahagan said in her best Monty Hall imitation.

CHAPTER 58

Stone arrived in Columbia Bay at 10 a.m. She accompanied Gahagan and a posse of federal and state law enforcement officers to McBride's home. As they pulled up, he was standing on the sidewalk leading to the front porch, the same spot where Matthews had stood when he had his final encounter with McBride.

"Don't tell me there's been another robbery," McBride laughed.

"Not exactly," Gahagan replied. "We're reexamining the first one."

"Oh," McBride said, surprised. An officer handed him a copy of the search warrant. Other officers filed by, walked up the sidewalk, and entered the house. Watching the parade of law enforcement, McBride asked, "Why have you come to my home?"

Gahagan ignored him. She was still fuming after being defeated in the court case. Convinced that McBride had robbed Matthews, she felt a miscarriage of justice had occurred on her watch. This was her opportunity to balance the scales.

Sensing Gahagan's contempt, McBride turned to Stone. "I hate to disappoint you, but I already stood trial for that robbery. I was acquitted. The last time I looked, there was a law against double jeopardy."

Having elicited no response from Stone, McBride turned back icily to Gahagan. "I recommend you order your troops off my premises. If not, I'll hit you with a lawsuit so big they're not going to be able to fit it inside the clerk's office."

Gahagan laughed.

"You think this is funny?" McBride glared at her. "I was acquitted because I was innocent. I was not inside that restaurant and I did not rob Sean Matthews."

"Nobody's retrying the robbery," Stone said calmly. "There's an investigation into the murder of Sean Matthews. People are looking at the Columbia Bay robbery with a fresh set of eyes.

"We don't think the robbery was committed to steal cash. The robbery was committed to retrieve a business card that Boris Prolokov inadvertently gave to Matthews."

McBride stepped backwards. "I have no idea what you're talking about."

"I think you do," Gahagan said.

Stone studied McBride's face, stoic and emotionless. She decided to probe, partly to satisfy her curiosity as to the extent of McBride's involvement. "You knew Prolokov," she began. "He called you after, Matthews arrived in Columbia Bay and told you about a business card he gave to Matthews that contained incriminating notes written on it.

"You may not have understood the significance of the notes, but you agreed to try to retrieve the business card. First you searched Matthews' hotel room. When that proved unsuccessful, you guessed the card was in his wallet."

McBride smiled wanly. "I do not have any idea what you're talking about."

"You traced Matthews to the restaurant," Stone continued. "When you saw the wad of cash, you figured you could fake a robbery. Your instincts probably told you that Matthews had come upon the money under questionable circumstances, so the likelihood of his reporting it to the authorities was slim."

McBride raised his hands. "Stop! This is insane. You've got the wrong guy. I need to talk with my lawyer."

But Stone kept talking. "You took the wallet to obtain the card inside of it. But before you could do that, you collided with Kevin Chalk. Next thing you knew, that card was suddenly on full display in a courtroom. You instructed your attorney to waive the admissibility of the contents of the wallet, betting no one would bother to study its items. Then, following your acquittal, you had your attorney move to seal the file to hide the information forever.

"But you still didn't have the card. So you accompanied Prolokov to Matthews' office on the 13th, and together the two of you murdered him."

McBride peered intently at Gahagan. "Are you such a sore loser as to subscribe to this kind of twisted logic?"

"I believe you were involved in Matthews' murder," Gahagan said. "And I believe we'll find evidence of the murder in your house."

As though on cue, a plainclothes officer came out of the house and walked over to where Stone, Gahagan, and McBride were standing. "We found the business card," he said.

Bewildered, McBride looked at the card held in the officer's latex-gloved hand. "I don't know anything about this," he said. "As God is my witness, I didn't rob anyone and I sure as hell didn't murder anyone."

"Save it for the jury," Gahagan said, relishing the words as she spoke them. She ordered that McBride be placed under arrest. An officer slapped a pair of handcuffs on him. Reporters, who had been summoned to the scene, swooped in, taking photos and film and sticking microphones in front of McBride, as he performed his perp walk to a waiting cruiser. Another officer palmed McBride's head like a basketball and stuffed him into the back seat.

Gahagan, with a look of keen satisfaction, got into the lead squad car to escort the suspect to the courthouse.

Stone watched as the cruisers departed. Despite the discovery of the business card, she detected a note of sincerity in McBride's voice. She suddenly felt a pang of doubt.

CHAPTER 59

Stone was seated on an embankment overlooking Columbia Bay when Katz called late in the day, shortly before sunset. "We just learned about the arrest," he said. "What are you doing?"

"I'm sittin' on the dock of the bay," she said, recalling a line from the classic song by Otis Redding and Steve Cropper. Her tone was melancholy. "Why, what's up?"

"I'm about to shock your system."

"I could use a good jolt right about now, to be honest."

"Here goes," Katz said. "If you remember, there were five individuals that Landry interviewed during his involvement with the BOM case. They included a hedge fund operator, an attorney, a state politician in Norfolk, and two businessmen, one of whom turned out to be Prolokov."

"Okay," she said, waiting for the punchline.

"The attorney on that list was Jon Bennett," Katz said. "At the time, he was with the Financial Crimes Information Network at the Treasury Department, collecting suspicious activity reports, or SARs, that contain information about illegal banking transactions."

Her mind raced over every bit of information she knew about Bennett, trying to connect dots. "I don't get it," she said. "What's the point?"

"Mac has done some more digging, and it turns out that Bennett was leaking SARs to Magellan. Landry must have figured it out and threatened to prosecute him. Bennett persuaded Landry to bury the evidence in exchange for orchestrating a sting operation for Landry's antiterrorist group.

"Bennett knew about Prolokov and his shady operations with Pasha Construction. So Bennett set up Prolokov as the stooge. It was an arrangement made in paradise. Landry got a score and a ton of publicity. Bennett got anonymity and freedom from prosecution."

"And Prolokov was left holding the bag," Stone said.

She stood and took a couple of steps toward the willows and underbrush that stretched to the water. The sun was setting. Red, orange, and yellow beams of light streaked across the western horizon. The heels of her boots slid into the soft murky earth.

Katz lowered his voice. "I also got a call from Jimmy Wolfe," he said. "Jimmy was with Bennett and Prolokov before you interviewed them. He told me that Bennett was more interested in knowing what Prolokov did after Matthews' murder than he was in providing competent legal advice."

"Meaning?"

"Meaning Bennett ran out to Prolokov's place to make sure the Russian wasn't going to implicate him in the murder."

"What about the recording that Matthews left for Hutton?" Stone asked. "How do you square that?"

"That was a hard one," Katz admitted with a sigh. "I racked my brain over how I knew about that conversation. Then it came to me. It was in Matthews' statement. I actually read it in your office while we were listening to the tape."

Stone recalled the other night when Katz mentioned how it bothered him, not knowing where else he had heard or read about Matthews' conversation with Hutton.

"The way I figure it," Katz said, "McBride didn't overhear anything at the restaurant, because he wasn't there. He got that information from Bennett."

"What do you mean?"

"After McBride was arrested, Matthews gave a statement to the police," Katz explained. "He provided that information in the statement. Gahagan then provided the statement to Bennett in discovery. Bennett, in turn, provided that nugget of information to McBride, probably with instructions to goad Matthews the next time he saw him."

"I – can't – believe – it," Stone said slowly, piecing things together. "So it's been Bennett all along."

"You need to test my theory," Katz said. "It isn't going to be easy. Gahagan is going to be royally pissed. We watched the perp walk. She wanted to make a big splash to get retribution against McBride. But she's got the wrong guy."

**

"As we parted, he said, 'By the way, Sean, did you buy any formal clothes at Columbia Bay or did the casual attire suffice?' Or something like that. That's what we were discussing in the restaurant that night. It's the only place he could have heard it."

Stone turned off the recording. She was seated in an interview room with Gahagan, McBride, and McBride's new attorney. It was late at night. Gahagan sat stoically beside Stone, whom she blamed for creating the difficult position in which she now found herself. Nonetheless, she reasoned, if McBride was innocent, her embarrassment for rushing to judgment was a small price to pay in exchange for catching the true murderer.

"I did have a conversation with Matthews and I did make that statement," McBride said. "I know this makes it sounds like I overheard their conversation at the restaurant, except that's not how it happened."

"Then how did you learn about that conversation?" Stone asked.

"Jon Bennett told me about it," McBride said. "It was included in Matthews' statement, which was part of the police report, or so he told me. After the acquittal, Bennett predicted Matthews would come by and apologize to me. He resented Matthews being so sanctimonious in the courtroom and recommended that I recite that conversation to infuriate the hell out of him.

"If I'd known Matthews was going to be killed, I never would have created a false impression like that. I mean, the man went to his grave believing that I was guilty, when I wasn't, you know."

McBride lowered his head. "I don't begrudge you for arresting me earlier today. Hell, I would have arrested me after listening to that."

Stone looked at Gahagan. McBride's statement jibed with Katz's surmise. "You shared the statement with Bennett as part of discovery, right?" she asked.

Gahagan nodded. "Naturally," she said. "Them's the rules."

"I never did anything," McBride said, his head still lowered. "Like I've said, I didn't rob anyone and I sure as hell didn't murder anyone. I hope you're now beginning to believe me."

Gahagan looked at Stone. "Then who robbed Matthews?"

"Process of elimination," Stone said. "Kevin Chalk."

Gahagan winced. "Son of a bitch."

Gahagan made arrangements for the police to bring in Chalk for questioning. As she did so, Stone sat alone with McBride and his attorney.

"What happened to your phone on the night you were arrested?" Stone asked.

"It was confiscated when I was taken into custody. Bennett retrieved it. At some point, he returned it to me."

"Not before he used it to call Prolokov," Stone said, disgusted. "Why did you retain this sleazebag?"

"I never did, not really," McBride explained. "He sort of appeared on the scene after my arrest. He visited me in my cell. He said something about being in the detention center visiting another client. I never questioned it. I just thought I was really lucky to have gotten him as my attorney."

"Were you in the D.C. area on the weekend of the 13th?" Stone asked.

"Yes, at Bennett's request. He called me late at night, after the news about Matthews' murder. He said there might be requests for interviews with people who might have had a motivation to harm Matthews. He said I might be a suspect and it would be in my interest to be available to be questioned. I did as he requested. But nothing came of it, and I returned home."

"When?"

"On the 17th. It was raining like hell. I didn't think the plane would get off the runway. The flight was harrowing. We rocked and rolled all the way to South Carolina."

Stone had one more question. "What about the business card that was recovered in your home?"

He paused, remembering. "You know, after I came up to D.C., I got a call from Bennett's office. They said they had some paperwork about sealing the court file that they wanted to give to me. I told Bennett's office I had a spare house key in the garage and they could drop it off at the house while I was still in D.C."

**

While Stone interviewed McBride, Katz phoned Hutton. "Do you remember when I asked you for the name of the person to whom you confided about the BOM settlement?" he asked.

"Of course," Hutton answered. "Don't tell me you want a second bite of the apple. If you do, motion granted, but only because you invited me to the celebration on the bridge, which I have to admit was pretty awesome. What's your guess?"

"Jon Bennett."

"You got it right this time," Hutton said.

CHAPTER 60

Shortly before midnight, an all-points bulletin was issued for Bennett.

Katz was on the phone with Stone, joined by White and Santana, getting the details about her meeting with McBride. When Stone finished, Katz provided them with a summary of the case as he now saw it. In many respects, he had reassembled the information originally uncovered by Stone.

"This started when Landry discovered Bennett was providing suspicious activity reports to BOM. To avoid prosecution, Bennett offered Landry a seemingly priceless jewel, namely an opportunity to arrest individuals plotting a terrorist attack in Washington, D.C.

"Landry concocted the plan to ship illegal arms up the Potomac, store them under the Wilson Bridge, and transport them to Anacostia in preparation for an attack against Joint Base Anacostia-Bolling.

"At some point, Landry shared the names of the missile systems being shipped up the river. Prolokov scribbled them on a business card. When Prolokov discovered the card was missing and in Matthews' possession, he contacted Bennett and told him that Matthews was going to Columbia Bay.

"Bennett enlisted a local yokel named Kevin Chalk, who decided to stage a robbery to retrieve the card. The robbery went awry when Chalk ran into McBride on the sidewalk. In a twist of fate, the business card became an exhibit in a criminal case.

"Concerned that someone would discover the names scribbled on the business card and uncover the plot, Bennett rushed to defend the man who was incorrectly accused of the robbery, McBride. After McBride was acquitted, Bennett moved to seal the file to hide the evidence in Carolina. Then he went to Northern Virginia to retrieve the card from Matthews.

"It's hard to know the circumstances that surrounded the retrieval effort, other than to say it went terribly awry and Matthews ended up dead.

"Bennett left Prolokov to clean up the mess that night. He kept the business card. But rather than destroy it, he used it to incriminate McBride by having someone plant the card in McBride's home.

"When Prolokov was charged with the murder, Bennett worked to get him out of jail because he needed the Russian on the bridge. When the operation imploded, Prolokov became a liability and Bennett knifed him the same way he butchered Matthews."

Stone paced back and forth as Katz explained the case. When he finished, she asked, "Do you think Bennett ordered the hit on David and me?" asked Stone.

"I doubt it," Katz said. "If Prolokov knew that you and David met with Alec Gordievsky, he would have instructed his associates to kill you. He probably planned to eliminate Gordievsky after the contraband had been loaded onto trucks at the bridge and hauled to the warehouse in Anacostia."

They sat silently in the room. Katz's phone vibrated. He looked at the screen and saw two new text messages.

One was from Gahagan, informing him that Kevin Chalk had confessed to robbing Sean Matthews. The other was from Bennett, who had learned about the issuance of the all-points bulletin. He had decided it was futile to run. Bennett said he was prepared to surrender tonight to Katz, alone, at Jones Point.

Katz shared the information with the others.

"What are you going to do?" asked White.

Katz looked at her. "I'm going to honor his request, of course," he said. "But first I'm going to arrange for some back-up. And I've got to make a phone call."

CHAPTER 61

Twenty minutes later, Katz parked his car at Jones Point. He could see Bennett standing on the pier. Katz got out of his car and walked slowly toward the killer. As he approached, he saw that Bennett held a semiautomatic in his hand.

"Who's that for?" Katz hollered. "You or me?"

Bennett laughed. "*Fatta la legge, trovato l'inganno.* I love that line. 'For every law, there is a way around.' How many judges and juries did you con with that line?" His face broke out in a broad grin. "A hundred? A thousand?" He staggered. "Are you still conning them to this day?"

Katz could smell alcohol on Bennett as he stepped onto the pier. The wooden landing tilted slightly. Katz and Bennett stood about five feet apart.

Bennett swayed. "I read about you online today. I expected the same story about an attorney sucking up to the political establishment to become U.S. Attorney. So pardon my surprise upon learning that you'd spent most of your professional career screwing the system. High praise, Mr. Katz. High praise."

"I got my job because I know my way around," Katz said bluntly.

"Put another way, it takes a thief to catch a thief," Bennett said. His speech was slurred. "It's the only way you could have detected my fingerprints in the case. My modus operandi must have triggered something in your memory bank. Whatever it was, bravo." He clapped, slapping an open palm against the wrist of the hand holding the firearm.

"It was the police report," Katz said. "I read Matthews' statement. If Steve McBride wasn't at the restaurant, as he swore, there was only one other way he could know about that information, and that was if you had told him.

"After that, it all pretty much fit into place. We had a lot of the facts, but they were pointing in the wrong direction, first at Prolokov and then at McBride. Fortunately, we got it right before you slipped through everyone's fingers."

Bennett waved the gun and mumbled, "The third one's the charm."

Katz disregarded the comment. "Why did you call me?" he asked. "What is it you want?"

"Freedom, Mr. Katz," Bennett said. "I understand aspects of the BOM case that you never uncovered. I am a valuable asset to you. I'm here to plea bargain for myself and secure a lenient sentence."

Katz guffawed. "Not for a double homicide. How about two life sentences? We'll agree to run them concurrently."

Bennett pursed his lips. "Not an unreasonable rejoinder, Mr. Katz. Understandable, I suppose, since one of the victims was a personal friend of yours, but hardly the response I would expect from a man like you.

"Of course, you'll be hard-pressed to convince a jury that Sean Matthews was murdered by someone other than Prolokov. And you'll find it equally difficult to turn Prolokov into a sympathetic victim in front of a jury."

Bennett staggered on the pier. "If I stood trial – which, understand, is not my preferred option – I have a good chance of being acquitted. My chances will be enhanced by the fact I'll have one of the best attorneys in the land." He smiled and pointed the barrel of the firearm at his chest. "Me."

His eyes watered. "I held no malice toward Matthews. I'm sorry it happened." Then his demeanor hardened. "It was different with Prolokov. Killing Boris was necessary, you understand. Kill or be killed."

Misty clouds formed above the water. Lights illuminated the white lattice-like bridge running across the Potomac. A cool breeze blew over the river. A car pulled into the parking lot and stopped next to Katz's vehicle.

Katz turned to the car. "Phil Landry's here," he told Bennett. Katz watched as Landry pulled a gun from a hip holster and held it in an outstretched position. Katz turned back to Bennett. "Put down your gun or he's going to shoot you." Then, in a louder voice, he hollered to Landry, "It's all okay, Phil. Bennett's surrendering. I have this under control."

"I don't think so," Landry replied as he stepped onto the pier. "Jon Bennett is a dangerous man."

Katz, Landry, and Bennett stood equidistant to one another. For a moment, the only sound came from traffic moving across the Wilson Bridge.

"He's dangerous, Mo," Landry repeated. "He's part of the terrorist cell we were tracking. I hoped he'd be on the bridge the other day so we could put the cuffs on him."

Bennett laughed. "A very convincing statement, Phil, but hardly the truth. I'm not a member of your so-called terrorist cell and I was never supposed to be on the bridge. I'm the guy who set the table, don't you remember?"

"What are you talking about?" Katz asked, playing dumb.

"Phil discovered my involvement in the BOM case and was going to arrest me, except I outwitted him," Bennett said, wobbling. "I offered up a sting operation in exchange for safe harbor and introduced him to a group of men anxious to wreak havoc on the nation's capital."

Landry took a step in Bennett's direction. "Shut up," he ordered.

"I don't think so, Phil," Bennett said. "I'll implicate you as an accessory after the fact. Too bad, but that's the way it goes." Then, in a conspiratorial tone, he said, "Phil maintained surveillance outside Matthews' office on the night of the murder. He did nothing to prevent the crime and took no action afterwards."

Bennett sneered at Landry. "They call you the ICBM behind your back because you're an insecure, conceited, bombastic, megalomaniac asshole. The mastermind behind Operation Open Sky. What a fucking joke! It was all a bullshit operation I concocted to avoid being implicated in BOM.

"Those guys weren't terrorists. They were hoods out to make a fast buck, nothing more. But you saw an opportunity to make the headlines. I was your set-up guy, but now I'm going to take you down."

Landry glared at Bennett and raised his gun level with Bennett's chest.

"Don't do it, Phil," Katz pleaded. "He's begging for a suicide by cop. Don't give him the easy way out."

Landry was not listening. He opened fire. A bullet struck Bennett in the stomach. Bennett reeled back and fell into the water. Katz leapt into the river after him. At the same instant, Santana and White emerged from the shadows and rushed toward the pier.

"He was going to kill Mo," Landry cried. "I couldn't wait any longer. I had to shoot."

CHAPTER 62

An emergency medical team arrived ten minutes later. By that time, Katz had pulled Bennett from the water and administered mouth-to-mouth resuscitation. Santana and White also rendered assistance, while Landry stood on the pier.

The bullet had passed cleanly through Bennett's midsection, missing vital organs. The EMTs summoned a helicopter, which landed in the parking area. As Bennett was airlifted to the Fairfax trauma center, squad cars began converging near the pier.

A crime scene perimeter was demarcated in yellow tape. Techs and forensic experts calculated the distance between the parties at the time the shot was fired. Law enforcement personnel stood around in clusters, jawboning about events of the past 24 hours.

Katz was cold, wet, and exhausted. Against his objections he was transported in an ambulance to Alexandria Hospital for observation. Santana accompanied him. White followed in a cruiser. As soon as he learned the news, Joey Cook sent out a blast email about what had happened. By the time the ambulance got to the hospital, McCarthy was waiting. Hutton and several members of the U.S. Attorney's office arrived minutes later.

"Bennett was a con artist par excellence," Katz told his compatriots as they huddled around his bed an hour later. "He conned Landry, Prolokov, Chalk, and a judge in Columbia Bay. He even incited Landry to shoot him."

"I'm glad he provoked Landry," Santana said. "Otherwise, Bennett might have taken out the two of you."

"I find it terribly ironic that you jumped into the water to save someone who killed your friend and probably would have killed you as well," Hutton added.

"Bennett wasn't going to shoot anyone at Jones Point," Katz said. "He wanted to work out a plea bargain. And the idea that Landry shot Bennett to save me is ludicrous. Landry shot Bennett to silence him, pure and simple."

"That's a bold statement," Santana said, lowering his voice. "You better consider the implications of that statement before you repeat it in public."

Katz grimaced as he repositioned himself in the bed. "Bennett was Landry's set-up guy for Operation Open Sky. I'll leave it at that."

"Then why did you alert Landry to the fact that Bennett was at Jones Point?" asked Hutton.

"You said Bennett was the only person with whom you discussed the BOM settlement," Katz said. "But Landry was the one who alerted Mac. The only way Landry could possibly have known was if Bennett called him.

"I needed confirmation that Landry and Bennett were working together. I figured the best way to get it was to have them confront one another. If I had known Landry was going to shoot Bennett, I never would have summoned Landry to join me."

The conversation continued for an additional thirty minutes. Everyone had an opinion to express or a question to ask. Eventually the nurses put an end to it. Katz was instructed to quit holding court and his entourage was ushered out the door. Ten minutes later, he was asleep.

**

Katz was released from the hospital at noon Tuesday. Snowe called as he sat in a wheelchair pushed by a hospital volunteer to an SUV waiting at the main entrance. Santana was behind the wheel of the vehicle.

Snowe's visit with her mom in Massachusetts was over. Her flight from Logan to Reagan National had been diverted to Charlotte. "I have a connecting flight late tonight to DCA," she said. "Can you pick me up? I can't wait to see you."

Katz rose from the wheelchair. Along the edge of the sidewalk, tall green grasses with white and red tassels swayed in the breeze with asters in bloom. He took a deep breath of cool, autumn air. "Stay where you are," he said. "We'll come and get you." He waved his thanks to the volunteer.

"There's no need for you to do that. And what do you mean, *we?* Who's with you?"

"Curtis," he answered, glancing at Santana as he climbed into the passenger seat of the SUV. "We need a break from the insanity." Santana nodded in agreement. "We'll drive straight down and rendezvous with you."

He lowered the phone. "Stoner's still in South Carolina, right?" Santana nodded again. Katz raised the phone. "Yeah, we're coming down to get you, and then we're going to the ocean. Don't you have a cousin in Charlotte you can hang out with for the afternoon?"

Snowe considered the idea. "Are you up for this?" she asked. "I mean, you're just being released from the hospital, right?"

"It's all good," Katz said. He hung up, and they took off. After brief stops at their respective homes to grab some things for the trip and at Meggrolls on Fayette Street to pick up a dozen crispy egg rolls, Katz and Santana headed south, stopping only to refuel.

They listened to music on the radio. Not satellite radio or streaming music, just whatever was available on the radio dial: rock, gospel, country, and soul. The songs included classics with legendary studio musicians from Muscle Shoals to Sun to Chess Studios. They sang along with most of the songs. And they devoured all the Meggrolls.

Thirty minutes north of Charlotte, Santana turned off the radio. "What happens next?" he asked. The question had been in the back of their minds the entire ride south.

"Assuming Bennett pulls through, he'll be charged with two murders," Katz replied. "A couple of important pieces of evidence link him to the crimes. One is Landry's watching him enter Matthews' law office on the 13th. The defense will fault Landry for failing to report the incident after it occurred, but I don't expect that'll hurt Landry's credibility.

"The second is Bennett's statement to me about the killings."

"What did he say, exactly?" Santana asked.

"He said he was sorry it happened and that he bore no malice toward Matthews. As to Prolokov, he said it was another story, kill or be killed."

"You think that's enough to convict?"

"Maybe, maybe not," Katz said, calculating the odds in his mind. "Which raises a question about the recovery of the knife used to kill Prolokov. If that knife is located and forensics links it to Bennett, it's over for him."

"I doubt anyone'll ever find it," Santana said. "Bennett's too smart."

"We'll see," Katz said. "Divers will comb the area off Jones Point. If the knife is located in close proximity to where Bennett was shot, it's going to be reasonable to conclude that he threw it in the water before Landry and I arrived."

**

They arrived in Charlotte around 7 p.m. Snowe was waiting at the airport. She and Katz got teary when they embraced as emotions bottled up the past few weeks found expression in each other's arms.

The threesome continued to their destination. Katz never stopped talking about the BOM settlement, the incident on the Wilson Bridge, Richard Bellows and his family, Lin and Reese, Landry, and Bennett's role in the murders.

CHAPTER 63

Night fell long before they arrived in Columbia Bay at the restaurant where Hutton and Matthews dined prior to the robbery. They found Stone at the bar. After a round of drinks, they sat at a table in the corner of the dining room, where they were soon served huge platters of seafood. Santana and Katz devoured the food as though they hadn't eaten for days.

"Truth is messy stuff," Katz said at one point, seemingly apropos of nothing. "It all seems simple enough until we're challenged to swear to it. Then it gets weighed down by consequence and interpretation. Sometimes it's best to just let it go by."

Santana looked at him with a crooked smile. They clicked glasses. Santana recalled their conversation in the hospital about Landry's motivation in shooting Bennett.

Stone smiled. She didn't have the foggiest idea what Katz was saying and had no desire to seek a further explanation. Sometimes Katz purposefully spoke in riddles.

Two hours later, the restaurant prepared to close. They were the only ones remaining; the bar and dining area were empty. The waiter brought the bill. Santana reached for his wallet, but Katz stopped him. "My treat," he said.

"Hopefully you're not paying in cash," Stone said.

Katz paid the bill with a credit card.

They walked out the door, across the sidewalk, and into the street, heading for the car. Clouds as thin as sheer curtains passed briskly overhead. Above the clouds, glassy stars cluttered the southern sky. A warm breeze squeezed between them, racing up the street. They lay arms across each other's shoulders and stepped in unison.

Once they got to the SUV, they all looked at one another and thought better of it. Santana called an Uber. The driver took them to the hotel where Stone had been staying. She had booked a second room for Snowe and Katz.

The couples said goodnight to one another and parted. The first thing Katz did when he got to their room was unpack three candles.

EPILOGUE

While recovering from his injuries, Jon Bennett was served with indictments for the murders of Sean Matthews and Boris Prolokov. His effort to mount a successful defense was cut short by the recovery of a serrated knife in the shallow water of the Potomac River off Jones Point. Forensics determined it was the weapon used to murder Prolokov.

Bennett adroitly pivoted from waging an aggressive defense to providing the F.B.I. with exhaustive information of his involvement in nefarious operations. The Bank of Magellan was not the sole beneficiary of suspicious activity reports that Bennett had surreptitiously shared during his tenure at the Treasury Department. Bennett's cooperation led to indictments at seven other financial institutions, creating a sensation in the financial community that rivaled the impact of Operation Varsity Blues in academic circles.

Bennett parlayed his cooperation into a plea in the Prolokov case with a recommended 20-year sentence. The court went along with the recommendation, and suspended half of it. After all, Prolokov was hardly a sympathetic figure in the eyes of the sentencing judge.

All charges against Bennett in Matthews' murder were dropped. Despite Bennett's statement to Katz at Jones Point, the attorneys handling the case concluded it would be hard to overcome the fact that all of the incriminating evidence pointed to Prolokov as the sole culprit. Landry remained mute and never acknowledged seeing Bennett at Matthews' office on the night of the 13th. Furthermore, the murder weapon in that case was recovered at Prolokov's home. No one was interested in pursuing the theory that Bennett planted the knife there just as he had engineered placing Prolokov's business card in McBride's home.

The perpetrators of the Wilson Bridge operation who survived the firefight were charged with a plethora of crimes, including the murders of the helicopter crew, conspiracy to bomb a place of public use, and interstate transport of explosives. Some were also charged with the attempted murder of Stone, Lin, and Reese, and the murder of the fisherman who inadvertently stumbled upon the operation. All but one of the defendants were sent away for life.

The exception was Alec Gordievsky, whose cooperation with the Alexandria Police enabled him to escape prosecution. His wife was permitted to emigrate from Russia. They moved to an undisclosed location in the U.S. under assumed names.

Lin recovered completely and she and Reese married shortly before she gave birth to a healthy baby boy. Reese continued working with Stone at the police department while completing law school. Following maternity leave, Lin returned to her duties at the U.S. Attorney's office.

An inquest was held into Landry's shooting of Bennett. Katz was the principal witness. He testified that Bennett appeared to be intoxicated and that he twirled and pointed a firearm in the moments preceding the shooting. Katz was never asked and he did not volunteer his opinion as to whether Bennett presented a clear and present danger to anyone at Jones Point. The inquest concluded Landry was justified in his use of force.

Judge Deale did not file a complaint against Landry for attempting to pressure her to release Prolokov. She presumed Landry would dispute the charge. Even if he didn't, he could argue that he felt obligated to get Prolokov to the Wilson Bridge to carry out the sting operation. Either way, Deale reasoned, Landry would win and it was not worth the bother.

Landry was hailed a hero for devising Operation Open Sky. A celebratory event was held in Alexandria, replete with tall ships sailing up the Potomac and through an open drawbridge on the Wilson Bridge. Over the objection of Senator Lowenstein, Landry was nominated as the new Secretary of the Department of Homeland Security.

Snowe's mother died in November and Snowe returned to Massachusetts to settle the estate. When she returned, she gave Katz an ultimatum: now or never.

Katz avoided committing to her by immersing himself in work. But time was running out there as well. Despite his successes, he was an anomaly as U.S. Attorney and it seemed unlikely he would remain in his position regardless of which party won next year's presidential election.

AUTHOR'S NOTE

The day after the May 31, 2019, shooting in Virginia Beach, while people are still absorbing its impact, I am signing copies of my first book "Daingerfield Island" at a Barnes & Noble at Potomac Yard in Alexandria, about 10 miles from my home. Corners of the globe touch in the aisles of this store. All walks of life move in harmony. People wearing jeans, flowing robes, hijabs, and suits and ties; heads adorned with flaming hair colors, arms displaying tattoos, faces defined by piercings; the young, the old, and the ageless. On their faces and in their gestures, I detect no anger, feel no resentment, and witness no prejudice toward others. In fact, I see the opposite: compassion, kindness, and human decency. I'm sure this positive vibe exists at the electronics store next door and the coffee shop around the corner, but it feels special here, in a bookstore, where people have come to seek, share, learn, explore, inquire, understand, and discover. The bookstore is the modern marketplace of ideas. Literature unites and inspires us. It expands our horizons. It instructs and teaches us. In each book I sign today, I affix a personal note of gratitude and appreciation for the shared values that bind us. There is madness, hatred, and resentment out there, but as long as we respect and care for one another, love prevails.

John Adam Wasowicz

ACKNOWLEDGEMENT

I am grateful to Linda Ely, Jim Crouch, Jim Drewry, Peggy McLaughlin, Maggie Wolff Peterson, and Daniel Baranowski for their comments and edits to the manuscript. Special thanks to Robin Herron, my wife; Charles Rammelkamp, my editor; and Clarinda Harriss, publisher of BrickHouse Books, for their meticulous work from start to finish. Additional thanks to Derek McGinty for narrating *Jones Point* and to Jim Cuddy and Matt Lynch for recording and producing the audiobook. As always, appreciation to our sons Alex, Andrew, and Aron for their inspiration, love, and support. And, finally, thank you for reading *Jones Point*. I hope you enjoyed it. If you have comments or suggestions, please email me at AlendronLLC@aol.com.

Elmo Katz will return in *Roaches Run*.

The audiobook version of *Jones Point* is available online for purchase through your favorite indie bookstore, book chain, retailer, or book distributor. The narration is performed by Derek McGinty, a popular radio and television personality who lives in Washington, D.C.